IN
QUIETNESS
&
TRUST

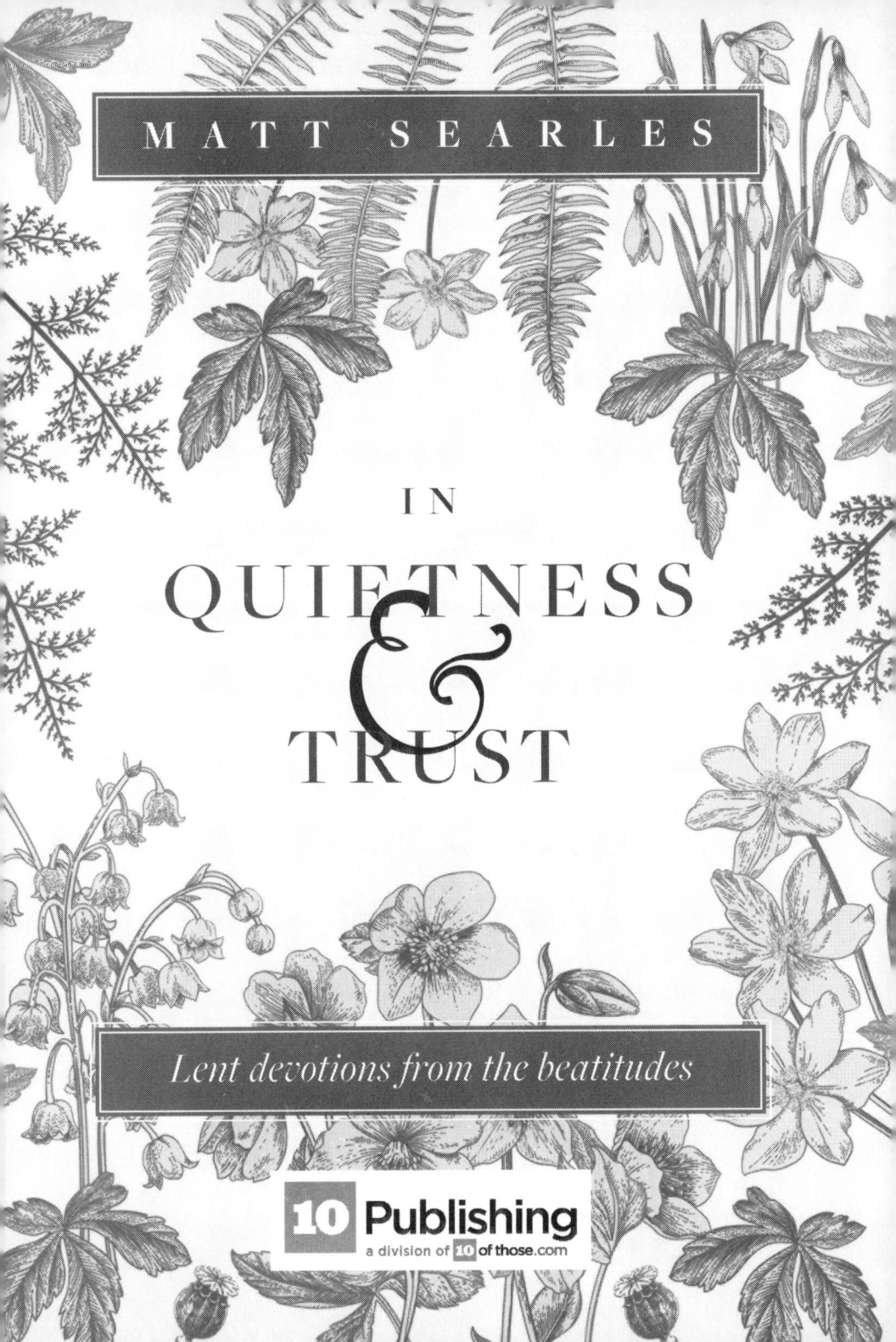

MATT SEARLES

IN

QUIETNESS

&

TRUST

Lent devotions from the beatitudes

10 Publishing
a division of 10ofthose.com

Copyright © 2024 by Matt Searles

First published in Great Britain in 2024

The right of Matt Searles to be identified as the Author of this Work has been asserted by him in accordance with the Copyright, Designs and Patents Act 1988.

British Library Cataloguing in Publication Data
A record for this book is available from the British Library

ISBN: 978-1-83728-0-278

Designed by Jude May
Cover image © Nata_Slavetskaya, mart_m | iStock

Printed in Denmark

10Publishing, a division of 10ofthose.com
Unit C, Tomlinson Road, Leyland, PR25 2DY, England
info@10ofthose.com
www.10ofthose.com

1 3 5 7 10 8 6 4 2

CONTENTS

INTRODUCTION

Since the early church, Lent has been celebrated as a period of 40 days (not counting the Sundays) to prepare for Easter. It has been a time of self-reflection, of pondering the need for the cross. As we reflect on our own neediness, we are reminded that being a Christian is not about earning anything from God, or trying to climb the spiritual ladder. The glorious blessings we have from God are received freely, through the work of Christ. We are not saved by our good works, or our religious performance – and this includes any Lent practice that we do.

Being a Christian is not seeking to ascend to God; rather it is a way *down*. We follow the way of Jesus, who went the way of the cross before resurrection. We follow the path of the seed, as Jesus himself said:

> Very truly I tell you, unless a grain of wheat falls to the ground and dies, it remains only a single seed. But if it dies, it produces many seeds. Anyone who loves their life will lose it, while anyone who hates their life in this world will keep it for eternal life (John 12:24–25).

These devotions will focus on the beatitudes from Matthew's gospel, beginning, 'Blessed are the poor in spirit...' These beatitudes exemplify this downward way: the way of quietness and trust. But the wonderful news is that this downward way is the *blessed* way. It is the way of flourishing.

So this Lent, let's spend time with Jesus in the wilderness. Let's join him on the downward way of the cross then resurrection; of the seed being buried in the ground before springing forth to abundant life. This is the path of our Saviour. This is the way of blessing.

This book has eight groups of five devotions, with each group focusing on the theme of one of the beatitudes from Matthew's gospel. Each day there is a verse or passage from Scripture with an accompanying devotion, a prayer and a song. The songs can be found online, but you can also find them on a Spotify playlist called 'In Quietness and Trust – Lent Playlist'.

These devotions have been written to be part of a liturgy for daily prayer, to give shape to our devotional time. (In the appendix there is an alternative liturgy, as well as some shorter prayers for when time is short.) It is suggested that you pray through this liturgy each day, either on your own or aloud with others, reading the devotion for the day at the appropriate point. If you are using the liturgy, it might be worth finishing the liturgy before you listen to the recommended song.

Because Sundays are not counted in the 40 days of Lent, it is not expected that you'll read one of these devotions on those days. However, if you would still like to do something on the Sundays, you may use the alternative liturgy in the appendix, with the accompanying 'Psalm of the day' reading plan. Also in the appendix you will find a bedtime liturgy, a pattern for a type of evening prayer called the Examen, brief guidance for the practice of heavenly meditation and also a suggestion for practising a time of silence, or 'micro-sabbath'.

But, of course, please use this book as is most helpful. You may just use the liturgy, or just use the devotions. You may choose to use some of the prayers, all of them or none of them. Don't worry at all if you get behind on the devotions, though once you are in Easter week, I suggest that you jump ahead to the final set of devotions, as these are focused on the events of Easter week.

However you use this book, my prayer is that within these pages there will be prayers, devotions and practices that might help you delight in our Saviour more, and spend time with him each day.

DAILY PRAYER LITURGY

The suggested pattern is that you use this each day, turning to the appropriate devotion for the day when you reach that part of the liturgy.

Call to worship

> One thing I ask from the LORD,
>> this only do I seek:
> that I may dwell in the house of the LORD
>> all the days of my life,
> to gaze on the beauty of the LORD
>> and to seek him in his temple.
> (Psalm 27:4)

A moment's silence may be kept to prepare our hearts.

Opening prayer

> Blessed are you, Lord Jesus Christ,
>> who walked the way of the cross
>> and said 'not my will but yours be done'.
> Grant us this lent season
>> to join you on this downward path
> So that we may know the life that is true life
>> and rejoice with you on resurrection morning.
> Amen.

Devotion for the day

Confession
If the meditation has not included a confession of sin, you may use one of the confession prayers from devotions 1, 3, 4, 8 or 29.

Words of assurance
> God so loved the world
>> That he gave his one and only Son
> That whoever believes in him shall not perish
>> But have eternal life.
> Therefore there is now no condemnation
>> For those who are in Christ Jesus.
> **(Adapted from John 3:16 and Romans 8:1)**

Prayers for the day ahead
A pause may be left before each 'we look to you', to give time to name before God particular needs for prayer.

> Heavenly Father, gracious provider
>
> *we look to you today.*
>
> For the strength for every good work
>
> *we look to you*
>
> For the putting to death of sin
>
> *we look to you*
>
> For the humility that befits your servants
>
> *we look to you*
>
> For a heart that seeks to gaze on your beauty
>
> *we look to you*

For help with the responsibilities we have

we look to you

For the things that worry and concern us

we look to you

For the care of our loved ones

we look to you

For the needs of our neighbours and our world

we look to you

We cast all our burdens on you Lord,
 Knowing that you care for us.
Amen.

Blessing

May the God of hope fill us with all joy and peace
 as we trust in him,
so that we may overflow with hope
 by the power of the Holy Spirit.
And may the grace of the Lord Jesus Christ,
 and the love of God,
and the fellowship of the Holy Spirit
 be with us all, evermore.
Amen.
(Romans 15:13 and 2 Corinthians 13:14)

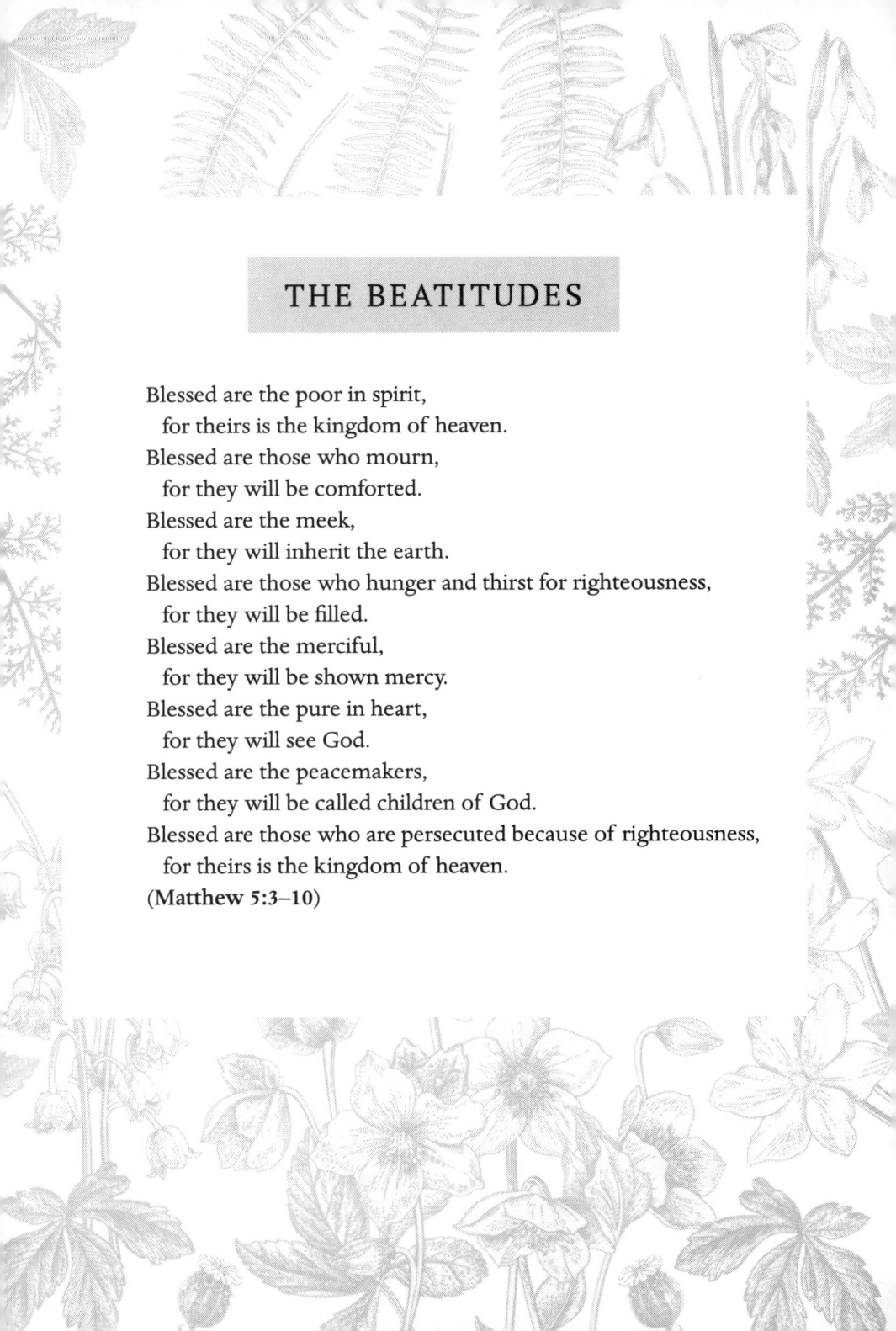

THE BEATITUDES

Blessed are the poor in spirit,
  for theirs is the kingdom of heaven.
Blessed are those who mourn,
  for they will be comforted.
Blessed are the meek,
  for they will inherit the earth.
Blessed are those who hunger and thirst for righteousness,
  for they will be filled.
Blessed are the merciful,
  for they will be shown mercy.
Blessed are the pure in heart,
  for they will see God.
Blessed are the peacemakers,
  for they will be called children of God.
Blessed are those who are persecuted because of righteousness,
  for theirs is the kingdom of heaven.
(Matthew 5:3–10)

THE POOR IN SPIRIT

DAYS 1–5

Blessed are the poor in spirit,
for theirs is the kingdom of heaven.

1

SEARCH ME, O GOD

Search me, God, and know my heart;
   test me and know my anxious thoughts.
See if there is any offensive way in me,
   and lead me in the way everlasting.
(Psalm 139:23–24)

Lent is traditionally a season where we ponder our sins that led Christ to the cross. It is a time of self-reflection, of pausing from busyness, of turning down the noise and chatter of life, and of being honest with ourselves and with God. Christians are always called to confess to God and say sorry for the wrongs we have done, but Lent is a particular season for this. The 40 days of Lent mirror the 40 years that Israel spent in the wilderness learning to rely on God, and the 40 days Jesus was in the wilderness being tempted.

The first beatitude is a wonderful place to begin our Lent journey. The first day of Lent (known as Ash Wednesday in some traditions) is a day of sorrow for our sin. Being honest about our sin is part of what it means to be poor in Spirit. When we confess our sins, we are acknowledging that we do not have the spiritual or moral excellence to earn anything from God. All that we have is by *grace*. When we confess our sins, we are reminded not just of our own spiritual poverty, but also of Christ's extraordinary generosity!

Confession is the way of *blessing*. Penitence is the path of flourishing. We admit we are empty, and Christ fills us. We confess we are unworthy, and we are given heaven.

So, this Lent season, let's take time to be open and honest before the Lord. Let's spend time allowing the Lord to search our very inmost being; not hiding, nor trying to cover our sins with fig leaves, but acknowledging our poverty of spirit. It won't always be easy. It won't always be comfortable. But it is the way of blessing.

Prayer

Search me, Christ, and know my heart
  Lord you know all our inmost desires and motives
  And to you there are no secret sins
  May I use this season to know my own heart better
  And open myself to your searching gaze
Test me and know my anxious thoughts
  I so readily fill my life with distractions
  And my thoughts run to and fro
  Grant me the rest that is only found in repentance
  And the peace of a heart fixed on you
See if there is any offensive way in me
  You call us to do justly, love mercy and walk humbly
  Yet so often I have failed in these areas
  Christ have mercy on me
  And conform me more into your perfect character
And lead me in the way everlasting
  Christ, you died daily on the way to Calvary
  and set your hope on joys to come
  May I take up my cross and join you on this journey
  So that I may also rejoice with you on resurrection morning

Song: *Rock of Ages* by The Choirs of Britain's Cathedrals

2

BLESSED ARE...

Blessed are the poor in spirit,
   for theirs is the kingdom of heaven.
(**Matthew 5:3**)

We've begun to think about what it means to be poor in spirit, but we mustn't skip too quickly over the first word of this (and every) beatitude. The first word of the beatitudes sums up what they are: *blessings*. This is what the name 'beatitude' means.

The beatitudes are not first and foremost calls to live a particular way. Rather Jesus is pronouncing blessings on a particular group of people. The beatitudes are *all* descriptions of followers of Jesus. Some of them are virtues that we might seek to grow in (for example, becoming more meek, hungering and thirsting more for righteousness), but fundamentally they are descriptions of all Christians.

Those who follow Jesus are blessed. Those who have taken up their cross are living the best way. Despite all that this world might value and celebrate, the life that is to be envied is the life of following Jesus. The way of Christ is the 'blessed' life: the flourishing life, the good life.

The second half of each beatitude explores what this blessing looks like. Followers of Jesus possess heaven, inherit the earth, are comforted and satisfied, will be shown mercy and are known as children of God. Although the full experience of these things will be in the new creation, all these blessings begin *now*! Jesus' way is not simply a way that leads to blessing; it is itself the blessed way to live.

The surprise of the beatitudes is that this blessed life, this flourishing life, is a 'downward way'. Being poor in spirit, mourning sin in the world and in our lives, seeking purity not riches, and so on – this is not the way that most people seek blessings. But Jesus points us to the glorious and paradoxical truth that this is the way of *life*. The way down is the way up. The way of giving is the way of receiving. The way of self-emptying is the way of being filled.

If you are a Christian, no matter how the world views you, no matter how you view yourself, Jesus' verdict on you is clear: you are *blessed*!

Prayer

The Lord bless us
   and keep us;
the Lord make his face shine on us
   and be gracious to us;
the Lord turn his face towards us
   and give us peace.
(**Adapted from Numbers 6:24–26**)

Song: *Blessing Song* **by Matt Searles**

3

THE JOY OF SALVATION

Restore to me the joy of your salvation (Psalm 51:12).

Confession of sin may not seem an obvious ingredient for a flourishing life. In society, admitting we have done wrong and apologising feels an increasingly outdated practice. In churches, weekly confession of sin may not be as common as it once would have been. Without the regular rhythm of corporate confession, it would be no surprise if confession were not a regular part of daily devotion for many Christians. Perhaps it is because confession of sin is seen as a negative thing. It is not part of the 'positive thinking' that we think leads to flourishing.

Psalm 51 is David's most famous prayer of confession. Notice that, for him, confession of sin is the way to know the joy of salvation. It is part of the privilege of being a child of God.

We don't confess our sins because we just want to beat ourselves up, or see ourselves as worthless. We confess our sins because we are of *great* worth: we are children of God, but children who err and stray like lost sheep, and so need to keep saying sorry. We do so, knowing that God loves to forgive, God loves to give his children fresh starts.

Being honest about our sins may be painful – it was for David in Psalm 51. Lent may not always be the most comfortable season. But it is the way of *life*. Hiding our sin is not the way to joy (Psalm 32:3–5). Pretending that we are better than we are leads only to exhaustion and disappointment.

Confession of sin is not simply admitting that we can't earn our way to God; it is also freeing ourselves of the burden of trying to! What joy and freedom there is in confessing our sin to God. We admit that we have done worse than we dare imagine, but knowing that we have a God who already knows the worst about us and loves to forgive.

We should be aware of our sin, but we must remember that it does not define us. Confession of sin is vital, not as an end in itself, but because of where it leads. Confessing our sins leads us to the joy of our salvation, because it leads us to our Saviour!

Prayer

Have mercy on me, O God,
  according to your unfailing love;
according to your great compassion
  blot out my transgressions.
Wash away all my iniquity
  and cleanse me from my sin.

For I know my transgressions,
  and my sin is always before me.
Against you, you only, have I sinned
  and done what is evil in your sight;
so you are right in your verdict
  and justified when you judge...

Cleanse me with hyssop, and I shall be clean;
  wash me, and I shall be whiter than snow.
Let me hear joy and gladness;
  let the bones you have crushed rejoice.
Hide your face from my sins
  and blot out all my iniquity.

Create in me a pure heart, O God,
  and renew a steadfast spirit within me.
Do not cast me from your presence
  or take your Holy Spirit from me.
Restore to me the joy of your salvation
  and grant me a willing spirit, to sustain me.
(**Psalm 51:1–4, 7–12**)

Song: *Have Mercy (Psalm 51)* by Caroline Cobb

4

HUMBLE AND CONTRITE IN SPIRIT

These are the ones I look on with favour:
  those who are humble and contrite in spirit,
  and who tremble at my word.
(Isaiah 66:2)

Lent is an opportunity to see ourselves rightly. A vital part of the downward way of flourishing is true humility: not thinking of ourselves more highly than we ought. So much of modern life consists in seeking to rise up, to ascend. We are told that blessing and flourishing are found in trying to be *more*. We are encouraged to present our best, idealised self to the world. Yet the way of Christ is the way of less. We humble ourselves before him. And he exalts us (1 Peter 5:6).

Pride is the opposite of poverty of Spirit. Pride is thinking that we have what it takes, that we have spiritual resources to draw on, so that (if we dare admit it) we don't need to rely fully on God. Pride is not just putting ourselves in the wrong place; it is putting God in the wrong place. We will never think of God rightly unless we also think of ourselves rightly. If I think that I'm big, that must mean I think that God is small. True blessing is found in the way of John the Baptist and what he said about Jesus: 'He must become greater; I must become less' (John 3:30).

Humility is the way of flourishing, because it is embracing reality, putting aside all pretence and self-deception. Humility isn't about being less human; it is being *more* human. We surrender our pride, and our personality shines through. We stop having to have everything *our* way, and discover the freedom of receiving life as a gift. We stop trying to justify ourselves, and rest secure in the one who justifies us.

God already knows everything about us, and he has already loved and accepted us in Christ, and made us his precious children. So we can surrender any pretence, and lay ourselves open before him. We have nothing to fear, nothing to hide.

Humility is the way of flourishing, because as we humble ourselves before him, he exalts us. We bring him our emptiness, and he fills us. We don't even deserve the crumbs under his table, but he gives us a seat at the feast.

Prayer

Lord Jesus, gentle and lowly
Deliver me from pride and grant me true humility:

From thinking much of myself

Lord deliver me

From looking down on others

Lord deliver me

From always wanting to get my own way

Lord deliver me

From craving the approval of others

Lord deliver me

From the fear of being criticised

Lord deliver me

From speaking too much and listening too little

Lord deliver me

From minimising my sin

Lord deliver me

From exaggerating my successes

Lord deliver me

From wanting to be well thought of

Lord deliver me

From thinking I can achieve anything without you

Lord deliver me

From making much of myself, and little of you

Lord deliver me

Amen.

Song: *Let My Words Be Few* by Matt Redman

FOR THEIRS IS THE KINGDOM OF HEAVEN

Scripture: Isaiah 61:1–3 (see opposite).

Right from the start, Jesus makes clear that his kingdom is not like any earthly kingdom. It is not the rich who are blessed and privileged, but the poor. It is not the powerful who are given a seat at the table, but the weak. It is not the elite who are let in, but the unworthy. This truly is good news!

But what *is* the kingdom of heaven (or the kingdom of God as it is called in the other gospels)? It is not a physical place, but it is where Jesus reigns. In the Old Testament, when there was a good king, *everything* was better. The people knew peace and prosperity; they ate and drank and were happy.

Jesus came as the king – the Christ or Messiah – to bring the kingdom of God. The glory days under Solomon are a pale reflection of the greater glories of Christ's kingdom. Christians will experience this saving reign of Christ fully and perfectly when Christ returns and ushers in the new creation, but we can be part of the kingdom of heaven now, as we know the blessings of being under Christ's rule. In Christ's kingdom, all that went wrong is being put right.

This is what is spoken of in Isaiah 61 (see opposite). These are words Jesus uses to introduce his own ministry (Luke 4:18), and words that provide a backdrop to many of the beatitudes. Jesus is restoring all things. And those who are welcomed to be part of this kingdom are not those who earn it, but those who know they can't: the poor in spirit.

The kingdom of heaven is unlike any other earthly kingdom, because Christ the king is so unlike any earthly ruler. The beatitudes show us what sort of king he is. One who blesses broken people. One who satisfies empty people. One who comforts broken people. One who gives beauty for ashes, and everlasting joy instead of disgrace.

Prayer

Read through Isaiah 61:1–3 slowly, thanking Christ for the character of the kingdom that he is bringing:

> The Spirit of the Sovereign LORD is on me,
>   because the LORD has anointed me
>   to proclaim good news to the poor.
> He has sent me to bind up the broken-hearted,
>   to proclaim freedom for the captives
>   and release from darkness for the prisoners,
> to proclaim the year of the LORD's favour
>   and the day of vengeance of our God,
> to comfort all who mourn,
>   and provide for those who grieve in Zion –
> to bestow on them a crown of beauty
>   instead of ashes,
> the oil of joy
>   instead of mourning,
> and a garment of praise
>   instead of a spirit of despair.
> (Isaiah 61:1–3)

Song: *Kingdom of God* by John Guerra

THOSE WHO MOURN

DAYS 6–10

Blessed are those who mourn,
for they will be comforted.

6

BLESSED ARE THOSE WHO MOURN

Blessed are those who mourn,
  for they will be comforted.
(**Matthew 5:4**)

I wonder if you've ever asked the question why there is such suffering in the world, and why often it seems to be some of the nicest and kindest people who suffer. I've certainly wrestled with these questions, and I know others will have too. Why is there so much injustice? Why do some of the kindest people suffer so badly? Why are there so many tears in this world?

I don't have any easy answers to these questions. And I know that when I'm struggling, I don't usually want 'easy answers' anyway. But I take comfort that Jesus expects his people to be asking such questions. He expects us often to find life very perplexing and hard.

This is what is in view in the second beatitude: 'Blessed are those who mourn.' The mourning here includes grief at the death of loved ones, but it is also broader than that. This is deep mourning at the way the world is, that things are not as they should be.

Jesus himself mourned. He wept as he looked over Jerusalem. He wept at the grave of his friend Lazarus. Jesus doesn't expect his people to breeze through life without a care in the world, but to mourn at sorrow, sin and suffering, just as he did. Tears may be the right response to the brokenness we see in the world.

In the next devotion, we'll think about the comfort he promises. But for now, let's stay with the mourning itself. Our tears are precious to our Lord. This is what David spoke about:

You keep track of all my sorrows.
  You have collected all my tears in your bottle.
  You have recorded each one in your book.
(**Psalm 56:8** NLT)

God sees your pain. God remembers your sorrows. He dignifies your tears. Mourning is sharing in the heart of God.

Prayer

This is a prayer that you might pray for people that you know who are struggling in various ways. You could even write it out and send it to someone, to let them know what you are praying.

> O Lord, Holy One of Israel,
>   helper of your people;
> Be with your servant [name],
>   as you have promised.
> May she not fear, for you are with her;
>   may she not be dismayed, for you are her God.
> Strengthen her and help her,
>   uphold her with your righteous right hand.
> Open up rivers of life in the desert places
>   and streams of blessing in the wilderness.
> May she rejoice in you, her redeemer,
>   and glory in you, Holy One of Israel.
> **(Adapted from Isaiah 41:8–20)**

Song: *Always Good* by Andrew Peterson

WEEP WITH THOSE WHO WEEP

Weep with those who weep (Romans 12:15 ESV).

Jesus was a man of deep joy, able to laugh with friends and enjoy all the good things of this world like food and feasting. But he also knew deep sorrow, not simply for what he himself faced as he bore our sins, but grief at the suffering of others. He wept over Jerusalem as he saw the city straying so far from God's ways, and knew all the sorrow this would lead to. He cried hot salty tears at the grave of his friend Lazarus, deeply moved at the grief of Mary and Martha.

Jesus calls us his followers to share in his empathy. He calls us to 'weep with those who weep'.

For many years I assumed that I should try to cheer up those who were weeping. At first, I tried to do this by being fun and upbeat. But as I spent more time in Scripture, this morphed into a 'spiritual' version: sending verses that were upbeat and joyful – but still trying to solve the problem of sadness and suffering. Of course there is a place for such verses, but over time I've been learning to be better at walking gently with those who suffer, and weeping with them, not trying to 'fix' them.

After my dad died when I was 20, the only card that I can remember is one where someone wrote a very short note saying how hard this must be, and that he was praying for me. The only conversation I can remember is with an older saint who gently told me of how he cried every day for two years when his wife died. Both men also taught me much about God over the years. But in that moment, they knew how to mourn, how to weep with me, and that was profoundly helpful.

Mourning is not a problem to be fixed, but a vital part of the Christian life. Being a Christian may mean that we weep *more*. Because walking the way of Christ means weeping with those who weep.

Reflection

What might it look like to weep with those who weep:

- among your family and friends?
- in your church?

Are there ways that your first instinct is to 'fix' rather than to weep with those who are struggling? Can you ask Christ to help you in this area?

Prayer

> Almighty and everlasting God,
>   the Comfort of the sad,
>   the Strength of sufferers,
> let the prayers of those that cry out of any tribulation
>   come unto Thee,
> that all may rejoice to find that Thy mercy
>   is present with them in their afflictions;
> through Jesus Christ our Lord. Amen.
> **– Gelasian sacramentary**

Song: *The Mercies of Christ* **by Matt Searles**

8

MOURNING OUR SIN

While Ezra was praying and confessing, weeping and throwing himself down before the house of God, a large crowd of Israelites – men, women and children – gathered around him. They too wept bitterly (Ezra 10:1).

Jesus pronounces a blessing on those who mourn, and this includes mourning for all that is wrong in the world, for things not being as they should be. Part of this mourning must therefore be mourning for our sin, as Ezra and the people model to us.

Mourning of sin is not simply being sad at any consequences that may arise from our sin, but mourning the sin itself. We are to feel the weight of it, the ugliness. God is good, and so rebellion against God is a rejection of what is good and true and beautiful, and an embracing of what is cruel, ugly and deceitful.

True sorrow for sin is a distinctly Christian practice. Because of the full and free forgiveness and cleansing offered in Jesus, we can be honest about our sins. We can ponder the horror and wickedness of the things we do that dishonour God, and hurt both others and ourselves.

Mourning sin is not casting doubt on the full forgiveness we have in Christ. Nor is it a statement of *identity* – we are not 'filthy sinners' but treasured children. But, as children, there is a need to feel the weight of our sin. Mourning sin means not minimising it, hiding it or excusing it. It means not distracting ourselves from it, but taking time to acknowledge it, and to feel its stain and shame.

The confession in the Book of Common Prayer (1662) models this mourning of sin. It speaks of how the memory of our sins should be 'grievous' to us, and the burden of them 'intolerable'. We need to sit a while with the weight of sin, to grieve over it. Such mourning of sin is always the way of flourishing, but Lent is a particular season for this. It is a time for deep and painful honesty and the laying down of our fig leaves, so that we may be clothed in the righteousness of Christ.

Prayer

Almighty God,
Father of our Lord Jesus Christ,
maker of all things, judge of all men:
We acknowledge and bewail our manifold sins and wickedness,
which we from time to time most grievously have committed,
by thought, word, and deed, against thy divine Majesty,
provoking most justly thy wrath and indignation against us.
We do earnestly repent,
and are heartily sorry for these our misdoings;
the remembrance of them is grievous unto us,
the burden of them is intolerable.
Have mercy upon us,
have mercy upon us, most merciful Father;
for thy Son our Lord Jesus Christ's sake,
forgive us all that is past;
and grant that we may ever hereafter
serve and please thee in newness of life,
to the honour and glory of thy Name;
through Jesus Christ our Lord. Amen.
– **From the Book of Common Prayer** (**1662**)

Song: *Lamb of God* **by Rachel Wilhelm**

THEY WILL BE COMFORTED

Blessed are those who mourn,
  for they will be comforted.
(Matthew 5:4)

I love having a God who cares about sorrows, who sees the 'little people', who treasures and bottles our tears. Just to know that he cares is balm for the soul. But the second half of the beatitude explores how this care is worked out in practice: he promises *comfort*.

Comfort is a word used in Isaiah 40–66 to summarise all of the blessing and restoration that God is bringing his people. God doesn't simply send us blessings from a distance. His comfort is intensely personal, as he himself draws near his people to bless them. God doesn't say 'don't cry'; rather he wraps us in his arms of love and holds us tight as we do pour out our tears.

Have you ever seen a parent dash to their child who has stumbled and cut their knee? Has your heart ever gone out to someone who is suffering, so you have moved towards them in love? Maybe you've known the experience of weeping uncontrollably, but strong arms have wrapped around you and a voice has said, 'It's ok, let it all out, I'm here, I've got you.'

These are just small pictures of the wonderful personal love of our God to us, his people.

He tends his flock like a shepherd:
  he gathers the lambs in his arms
and carries them close to his heart;
  he gently leads those that have young.
(Isaiah 40:11)

Some people naturally move away from those who are suffering. It will be too costly. It will take time and effort. It might just be unpleasant to think about. I know at times I've acted this way. Not so with God. He moves towards those who suffer – even if it costs him. Why was Jesus born? Why did Jesus die? So he could be our comforter.

Prayer

Jesus our comforter,
  We come to you
When we are tired and weak
  We come to you,
When weighed down by sin
  We come to you,
When hemmed in by trouble
  We come to you,
When burdened by sadness
  We come to you,
When we cannot see the way to go
  We come to you,
Jesus our comforter,
  Abide with us today.

Song: *Comfort, Oh Comfort* by Caroline Cobb

10

NO MORE TEARS

I heard a loud voice from the throne saying, 'Look! God's dwelling-place is now among the people, and he will dwell with them. They will be his people, and God himself will be with them and be their God. "He will wipe every tear from their eyes. There will be no more death" or mourning or crying or pain, for the old order of things has passed away' (Revelation 21:3–4).

When he writes to the Thessalonians, Paul reminds them that Christians do not grieve like the rest of the world, who grieve without hope. Jesus died and rose again, and he will also raise Christians who have died in him. Jesus' resurrection is the pattern for all Christian believers.

But as well as being the pattern for our individual lives, Jesus' resurrection is also the pattern for all of creation. The whole world will be resurrected. This means that 'mourning, but with hope' applies to *all* mourning: mourning our sin, mourning the state of the world, mourning the brokenness we see. God is restoring *all things*. This is the wonderful truth celebrated in Revelation 21. When Christ returns there will be no more tears, because all reasons for tears will be gone.

Part of living the Christian life is setting our sights and our hearts on this future reality. Part of mourning now involves not just sadness at how things *are*, but a yearning and a longing for how they will be. Christ will return. We will see our Saviour face to face. We will dwell with him for ever in a perfect world of love. We know how the story ends. And so we are sustained for the journey.

In the words of the Puritan Richard Baxter:

> Yonder is the region of light; this is a land of palpable darkness. Yonder twinkling stars, that shining moon, the radiant sun, are all but as the lanterns hanged out at thy Father's house, to light you while you walk in the dark streets of the earth: but little do you know (ah, little indeed!) the glory and blessed happiness that is within![1]

Suggested practice: heavenly meditation

If you wish to meditate more on heaven, you may wish to use the 'heavenly meditation' practice found in the appendix at the end of this book.

Prayer

> Almighty and everlasting God,
>   Creator of the ends of the earth
> Who never grows tired or weary
>   And whose understanding no-one can fathom
> We wait for you
>   when we are feeling weary
> We wait for you
>   renew our strength
> May we rise on wings like eagles
>   May we run and not grow weary
>   May we walk and not be faint
> Everlasting God, we wait for you.
> (**Adapted from Isaiah 40:27–31**)

Song: *We Will Feast in the House of Zion* **by Sandra McCracken**

THE MEEK

DAYS 11–15

Blessed are the meek,
for they will inherit the earth.

BLESSED ARE THE LITTLE PEOPLE

Blessed are the meek,
   for they will inherit the earth.
(**Matthew 5:5**)

Like the first two beatitudes, this third beatitude is first and foremost a pronouncement of blessing, not a call to action. The word 'meek' doesn't just refer to a virtue of humility; the primary meaning is 'those who are in a hard or vulnerable situation' – in other words, the 'little people'.

Every society has 'little people': people who are seen as less than others. Often it is the poor, or the elderly. Often it is people with mental or physical health struggles, those who are less able to be 'productive members of society'. Maybe it is those who are different in some way from the majority.

Sadly, churches can work in just the same way. Even in church, people may be valued according to what they can contribute, by what gifts they have (and the health struggles they don't have).

A friend was speaking to me recently about his mental health struggles and how they made him feel. He gave the analogy of feeling like a 'dented tin'. He spoke of how everyone, when shopping to buy tins (such as of beans), picks the ones without dents; no-one wants dented tins. He said that he felt like a dented tin. He thought no-one would want him, or think he had anything to contribute. So he believed he would be left on the shelf, unwanted, unvalued. It was incredibly moving and sad to hear him speak this way – though I knew something of how he felt. Maybe at times you too have felt like a dented tin.

The good news is that our God does not work like this. God does not value the 'little people' as less – in fact he pronounces blessing on such people! Read the Bible and see how often he uses widows, foreigners, the poor, the powerless to advance his kingdom. Read through the Bible and you will *never* see an example of God favouring the strong.

Jesus cares about little people. Jesus *uses* little people. When he sees a dented tin, that's the one he moves towards.

Prayer

In confidence of your goodness and great mercy,
　O Lord, I draw near to you,
　　as a sick person to the healer,
　　as one hungry and thirsty to the fountain of life,
　　a creature to the creator,
　　a desolate soul to my own tender comforter.
Behold, in you is everything I can or ought to desire.
You are my salvation and my redemption,
　my hope and my strength.
Make my soul rejoice in you today
　for to you, O Lord, have I lifted up my soul. Amen.
– **Thomas à Kempis**

Song: *All the Poor and Powerless* by **All Sons and Daughters**

HE MUST INCREASE, I MUST DECREASE

John replied ... 'I am not the Messiah but am sent ahead of him. The bride belongs to the bridegroom. The friend who attends the bridegroom waits and listens for him, and is full of joy when he hears the bridegroom's voice. That joy is mine, and it is now complete. He must become greater; I must become less' (John 3:27–30).

The story is told of when Alexander the Great met the philosopher Diogenes. Alexander was anything but meek, and offered to grant Diogenes anything he wished. Perhaps he thought Diogenes would ask for some gift, or some favour from the great man. Diogenes' reply was simple: 'Stand a little to the side, you're blocking the sun.'

This story captures what John the Baptist was all about. He was meek. He didn't put himself forward, rather he wanted Jesus to be central. He stood to one side, so as not to block the sun.

John's words above were prompted by his disciples noticing that Jesus and his disciples were baptising more people than they were. Perhaps they were envious of the attention that Jesus was getting. Perhaps they wanted a little more of the spotlight.

Not so with John the Baptist. He knew that Jesus was the bridegroom, and he had just a supporting part: the friend who attends the bridegroom. No best man or usher seeks to upstage the bridegroom on the wedding day. Similarly, John didn't see his role as to push himself forward, but to stand to the side so that Jesus could be central.

This is the pattern for all disciples. Christ must become greater; we must become less. We have a glorious role to point to Christ, but often this means stepping to the side so that we don't block the sun! If people's eyes are on me, they can't be on Christ.

I find this a challenge, as I want people to think well of me. I want people to speak well of me. But true meekness says 'not me, but Christ'. It is not thinking we are without worth – far from it – but it is recognising our place. Christ is at the centre. He is the bridegroom. Let's not seek to be honoured, but let's want Christ to be honoured. Let's stand to the side so our world can see the sunshine of his goodness and glory.

Prayer

O omnipotent Father,
  God of truth, God of love,
permit me to enter into the cell of self-knowledge.
I admit that of myself I am nothing,
  but that all being and goodness in me comes solely from You.
Show me my faults, that I may detest my malice,
  and thus I shall flee from self-love
and find myself clothed again
  in the bridal robe of divine charity,
which I must have in order to be admitted
  to the wedding feast of life eternal.
– **Catherine of Sienna**

Song: *Yet Not I But Through Christ in Me* **by CityAlight**

13

BLESSED ARE THE GENTLE

Take my yoke upon you and learn from me, for I am gentle and humble in heart, and you will find rest for your souls (Matthew 11:29).

When Jesus pronounces blessing on the 'meek', this word doesn't only mean 'humble' but also 'gentle'. Gentleness is a fundamental characteristic (virtue) of an authentic disciple, because it is such a central description of Christ's character.

Jesus used his power *for* others, never against them.

Jesus used his words to build up, not tear down.

Jesus was careful never to break a bruised reed (which presumably means he took the time to learn where people were bruised and vulnerable).

Jesus never snuffed out a smouldering wick, but encouraged and built up those who were struggling.

The example of Jesus gives a beautiful picture of gentleness for us to follow. And Jesus shows us that gentleness is not weakness. Rather it is strength used for the good of others. To put it another way, it is a refusal to use our strength to our own advantage (often pushing others down in the process). It is those who have the *most* power and influence who should hear this call to gentleness the most forcefully. This beatitude is not about keeping the weak and powerless in their place.

Gentleness is at the very heart of Christlikeness. There is no holiness without gentleness. Let us all seek to grow in this wonderful virtue, as we follow the example of our gentle, gentle Saviour.

Prayer

Gentle Lord,
You tend your flock like a shepherd
  and gather the lambs in your arms
You carry them closely to your heart
  and gently lead those that have young
You are near to the broken-hearted
  and you bind up their wounds
Grant that we, who bear your name
  may also bear your gentle character
Give us tender hearts
  gentle hands
  eyes to see pain
  and feet that move towards those in need.
(Inspired by Isaiah 40:11 and Psalm 147:3)

Song: *With Great Gentleness* (from *Steadfast Live*) by Sandra McCracken

14

A QUIET AND CALM SOUL

My heart is not proud, LORD,
  my eyes are not haughty;
I do not concern myself with great matters
  or things too wonderful for me.
But I have calmed and quieted myself,
  I am like a weaned child with its mother;
  like a weaned child I am content.
(**Psalm 131:1–2**)

Our modern society pushes us to know all things, understand all things and be able to control all things – and technology only exacerbates this, promising to remove our creaturely limits from us.

The psalmist celebrates being small. The picture is of a baby who is content. Not a newborn who is constantly crying and fussing for food, but a baby who has been weaned onto solid food, and so is able to rest contentedly at her mother's breast.

The psalmist doesn't need to know all things. He doesn't need to understand all things. He certainly doesn't need to be able to control all things. He is content with being small – knowing he rests at the breast of a God who is very big!

All sorts of worries, thoughts and concerns present themselves to our minds on a daily basis. I certainly know the experience of all my attention being drawn to one situation that I just can't understand, or to a problem I can't fix (though I keep myself awake at night planning how I might do so).

For the psalmist, what is, *is*. He's not focused on all he wants to be different, he's not constantly analysing everything. He's not engaging his problem-solving brain in all aspects of life, as if life itself is a problem needing solving. He is meek. He is small.

We have a big God, so we should be prepared to be small. We have a God who is in control of all things – working all things for our good! – so we don't need to be in control of everything.

Optional prayer exercise

If it is comfortable for you, you may wish to consider some difficulty or problem that is going on for you at the moment. Don't pick anything too difficult or painful – just something that you're comfortable staying with for a while. Instead of praying a long prayer (which may be an opportunity for the 'problem-solving brain' to kick in and lead you to think more about the situation), try praying a very *short* prayer, then leaving the situation with God. If the problem presents itself again, you may choose to repeat the short prayer, and again choose not to engage your problem-solving brain. Use the short prayer to commit the situation to God (or, rather, remind yourself that you already have committed it to God!).

Here are some short prayers, sometimes known as 'breath prayers', that you may choose to use:

Lord, into your hands.

Father, your will be done.

I do not know what to do,
   but my eyes are on you.

The aim of this practice is to help us learn the habit of choosing not to engage our problem-solving brain, but rather leaving situations with God.

Song: *O Lord, Hear My Prayer* **by Simply Taizé**

15

THEY WILL INHERIT THE EARTH

See, I will create
   new heavens and a new earth.
(**Isaiah 65:17**)

As Christians, often we use shorthand and speak of going to 'heaven' when we die – referring to the spiritual reality where God dwells. But, in fact, we await a new heavens and a new earth. Jesus doesn't save his people out of this physical world for a purely spiritual existence. Rather he is redeeming and resurrecting this physical world. We look forward to a renewed creation. We look forward to a day when heaven and earth will be united: when the dwelling place of God will be among his people.

It's vital for us as Christians to see our future rightly. Our future is not a disembodied existence, floating around on clouds; rather it is a glorious new creation, perfectly ruled over by Christ. All that Adam and Eve lost will be restored. All that creation should have been, will one day be reality. Salvation in Christ is not some 'plan B'. All God's creation plans are being fulfilled.

This is particularly important as we think about meekness. In this world, the pushy and the aggressive are often the ones who prosper. Christ's response is not to say, 'Leave the world to them, I'll give you spiritual things instead.' Rather, those who trust in Christ will receive heaven *and* earth! Think of all the good things of this world – music, creativity, friendship, food, our bodies. These all belong to Christ, are redeemed by Christ and one day will be the possession of Christ's people!

A few years ago, there was a trend for books with titles like '1000 Places to See Before You Die' or '1000 Books to Read Before You Die'. The Christian response is not to say 'I don't care about those things – I only care about spiritual things', nor is it to chase after them all. Instead, we can say 'these are part of Christ's good creation, and one day they will all be mine, as together with Christ I inherit the earth'. This is the perspective that enables us to be meek in the here and now. This is the perspective that enables us to join Christ on the downward way. One day all things will be mine. We never need to have any fear of missing out in this life.

Prayer

Lord Christ, what riches await us!
  Help us fix our eyes on glories to come:
Where the mountains will drip with sweet wine
  and the forests and valleys will resound with singing
Where we will feast with you for ever
  and drink with joy from your well of salvation
Where the blind will see and the lame will dance
  the desert will bloom and the wilderness rejoice
Where you will bestow on us a crown of beauty instead of ashes,
  the oil of joy, instead of mourning,
Where gladness and joy will overtake us,
  and sorrow and sighing will flee away.
When all the nations on earth join together
  in ceaseless praise to you
And you will be our all in all.

Song: *The Year of His Favour (Isaiah 61)* by Caroline Cobb

A HUNGER FOR RIGHTEOUSNESS

DAYS 16–20

Blessed are those who hunger and thirst for righteousness,
for they will be filled.

16

SEEK FIRST HIS KINGDOM AND RIGHTEOUSNESS

Blessed are those who hunger and thirst for righteousness,
  for they will be filled.
(Matthew 5:6)

> Seek first his kingdom and his righteousness, and all these things will
> be given to you as well (Matthew 6:33).

Hunger and thirst are some of the most primal emotions, reflecting our most basic needs. Whatever else we have, if we don't have enough food and water, we can't survive. Jesus takes these very powerful images of hunger and thirst and applies them not to food and drink, but to *righteousness*. There is a blessing on those who long for righteousness as much as they long for food itself.

In Matthew's gospel, the word 'righteousness' tends to be used as a synonym for godliness; it describes moral *behaviour*. (We may be more used to Paul's letters, where it refers more to the perfect *status* we have, given to us by Christ.) Hungering and thirsting for righteousness means wanting God's will to be done, in our own lives and in wider society.

Believers are those with a new heart and new desires. We might even say that we have new *needs*. For a Christian, the basic necessities of life should now not only include food, shelter and clothing, but also walking God's way. I confess that I'm not used to thinking this way. I can so often see pursuing holiness as something of an optional extra. It falls into the 'nice to have' category rather than the 'need' category.

If we want to flourish in life, we can't do without food and drink. Without them our body can't survive. So too, if we want to flourish spiritually, we must pursue righteousness. As John Stott put it: 'There is perhaps no greater secret of progress in Christian living than healthy, hearty spiritual appetite.'[2]

Prayer

Grant me, even me, my dearest Lord,
  to know you, and love you, and rejoice in you.
And, if I cannot do these perfectly in this life,
  let me at least advance to higher degrees every day,
  till I can come to do them in perfection.
Let the knowledge of you increase in me here,
  that it may be full hereafter.
Let the love of you grow every day more and more here,
  that it may be perfect hereafter;
  that my joy may be great in itself, and full in you.
I know, O God, that you are a God of truth,
O make good your gracious promises to me,
  that my joy may be full. Amen.

– **Augustine**

Song: *Take My Life and Let It Be* **by Paul Zach and Liz Vice**

17

DELIGHT IN HIS COMMANDMENTS

Blessed are those who fear the LORD,
   who find great delight in his commands.
(**Psalm 112:1**)

Our relationship to God's commands tells us a lot about our relationship with God himself. Psalm 112 (you may wish to read all of it) celebrates the blessing on the one who *delights* in God's commands. To such a person, God's commands are not burdensome; they are not 'rules that we follow because we have to, even though we'd rather not'. Living God's way is a delight, it is the way of *blessing*.

Maybe we're not used to thinking of God's commands this way. I was surprised when I first saw that the very first commandment in the whole Bible is presented as a *blessing*: 'God blessed them and said to them, "Be fruitful and increase in number; fill the earth and subdue it"' (Genesis 1:28).

When Moses gave the law in Deuteronomy, the commands and laws are described as being given 'for your own good' (Deuteronomy 10:13).

I admit that this isn't often how I think about God's commandments. I naturally resent anyone telling me what to do, thinking that it will probably curtail my fun or limit my freedom. I sometimes assume that it is like that with God's commandments: perhaps God is just laying burdens on me, trying to spoil my fun.

I need to remind myself that God is good, and so what he commands us is good. What he commands us is for *our* good! God really wants us to live whole, flourishing lives. God's laws to us are not just things we need to 'grin and bear', but things we can increasingly delight in.

Of course this won't always be how it feels. But that's where we need to remember the character of God. He is good, and his intentions for his children are good. He lovingly teaches us the blessed and best way to live. Ultimately, we can delight in God's commands because we delight in God himself.

Prayer

O sacred heart of Jesus,
  fountain of eternal life,
Your heart is a glowing furnace of love.
  You are my refuge and my sanctuary.

O my adorable and loving Saviour,
  consume my heart with the burning fire
  with which yours is aflamed.
Pour down on my soul those graces
  which flow from your love.
Let my heart be united with yours.
  Let my will be conformed to yours in all things.
May your will be the rule of all my desires and actions.
Amen.
– St Gertrude of Helfta

Song: *Empty Me Out* **by Liz Vice**

O LORD, HOW LONG?

O LORD, how long shall I cry for help,
  and you will not hear?
Or cry to you 'Violence!'
  and you will not save?
(Habakkuk 1:2 ESV – you may wish to read verses 2–4)

Part of walking God's way will involve caring about the things that God cares about. The prophet Habakkuk saw the violence and injustice all around him, and so cried out in anguish: 'O LORD, how long?'

Perhaps we are used to thinking of the contentment that we know in the Christian life (Philippians 4:11). But there is also a holy and good *discontentment*. We care when God's ways are not lived out, when wicked people prosper and the righteous suffer. Those who are supposed to deliver justice for the weak and oppressed often fail to do this, sometimes for their own personal gain. There is a gaping gulf between how our world works and how God wants people to behave.

This is what makes Habakkuk's cry so anguished. He knows that God is good, but God doesn't seem to be acting, or even hearing his prayers. Injustice seems to have the upper hand. Maybe you've experienced a time like this and the pain that it brings. Habakkuk is living in the gap between what he knows about God's character and what he sees all around him. So, his cry is 'how long?' This is not a cry of unbelief, but *faith*.

Habakkuk hungers and thirsts for righteousness. Our Saviour, Christ, hungered and thirsted for righteousness. And we should too. Perhaps for some of us, that means being *more* heartbroken at what we read in the news or hear happening around us. Even if our own current situation happens to be comfortable, we should still share this heartbreak at destruction and violence, at oppression and injustice.

Like Habakkuk we should earnestly pray, 'O Lord, how long?' In fact, this is what we are doing when we pray 'your kingdom come'. A mark of being a follower of Christ is longing for his reign of truth and justice, of hungering and thirsting for righteousness.

Prayer

How long, O Lord, will violence fill our land?
And people war against their fellow man?
Break down the walls of hatred and pride
Let justice like a flowing stream arise
Have mercy, Lord! Dispel the deeds of night
And shine on us your Saviour's light.

How long, O Lord, will nations rage in vain?
And rise against your sovereign rule of grace?
How long will Jesus Christ be denied
Until his coming brightens all the sky?
Have mercy, Lord, 'til Christ returns as king
And treads all evil underneath his feet.

How long, O Lord, will those who love your name
Be silent when this world is filled with pain?
Give us the grace to speak your truth
And answer every evil deed with good
Have mercy, Lord! Our hope is in your word
Send out your gospel truth in all the earth.

Song: *Have Mercy, Lord* by Matt Searles

(which is the words above set to the tune of 'O Come, O Come, Emmanuel')

19

LET JUSTICE ROLL

Let justice roll on like a river,
    righteousness like a never-failing stream!
(**Amos 5:24**)

The church has long celebrated the prophets as wonderful examples of those who hunger and thirst for righteousness. Amos condemns the people for their religious practices which are all for show, and aren't worked out in how they treat others. A mark of being in right relationship with God is to desire the things that he desires. We are not saved by longing for justice and righteousness, but longing for justice and righteousness is the *fruit* of being saved!

Right relationship with God was *always* to be worked out in practical ways. Love for God always led to love for neighbour.

This is why James could say (with the characteristic boldness of Jesus himself): 'Religion that God our Father accepts as pure and faultless is this: to look after orphans and widows in their distress and to keep oneself from being polluted by the world' (James 1:27).

Part of hungering and thirsting for righteousness will involve actively pursuing justice and righteousness, particularly for those who are needy. This is just what our God is like. We have a God who poured himself out for the needy – and we love him for it! These verses shouldn't be seen as a burden, but an opportunity – remembering that whatever we do for those in need, we do for our Saviour Jesus himself.

Surely we want a God who cares about injustice. Surely we want a God who does not turn a blind eye to oppression and violence. Surely we want a God who sees what happens in the dark, who cares about it and who will do something about it. God is not indifferent to injustice, he is not deaf to the cries of the poor and the oppressed. And we, his church, are called to share in caring about what he cares about.

Reflection and prayer

As you read the passage below from Isaiah, you might wish to pause every verse or few verses and:

- Pray 'Lord, help me to hunger and thirst for this sort of righteousness'
- Consider what putting this verse into practice might look like
  - ~ for you personally
  - ~ for your church
- Ponder how Jesus himself perfectly lived this out.

> Is not this the kind of fasting I have chosen:
> to loose the chains of injustice
>   and untie the cords of the yoke,
> to set the oppressed free
>   and break every yoke?
> Is it not to share your food with the hungry
>   and to provide the poor wanderer with shelter –
> when you see the naked, to clothe them,
>   and not to turn away from your own flesh and blood?
> Then your light will break forth like the dawn,
>   and your healing will quickly appear;
> then your righteousness will go before you,
>   and the glory of the LORD will be your rear guard.
> Then you will call, and the LORD will answer;
>   you will cry for help, and he will say: here am I.
>
> If you do away with the yoke of oppression,
>   with the pointing finger and malicious talk,
> and if you spend yourselves on behalf of the hungry
>   and satisfy the needs of the oppressed,
> then your light will rise in the darkness,
>   and your night will become like the noonday.
> (Isaiah 58:6–10)

Song: *Let Justice Roll* **by Sojourn Music**

20

THEY WILL BE SATISFIED

...they shall be satisfied (Matthew 5:6 ESV).

Much of modern life is spent in the pursuit of some goal. We have some vision of the 'good life' that we strive for, hoping that, if we reach it, we will be happy and content. But often we are either unable to reach that goal or, when we do reach it, it doesn't actually deliver what we hoped it would. Dissatisfaction is a well-known feeling in our society, as is its sister emotion, disappointment. We don't need to have lived for long to learn caution about pinning our hopes too much on any one thing; we still bear the wounds of disappointment from past experiences. Perhaps we have a similar caution when it comes to following Jesus.

But Jesus promises that those who hunger and thirst for righteousness *will* be satisfied. If we seek after God, we *will* find him. If we make him our greatest treasure, we *will* find that desire to be met, in a far deeper and more satisfying way than we could ever imagine. When we come to Jesus, we will never ultimately be disappointed.

We will know this deep satisfaction fully and perfectly when we see our Saviour face to face, and enter into his eternal bliss. But we can know this satisfaction *now* also, as God dwells within us by his Holy Spirit. God is not distant; he is a personal God who came to earth as Immanuel, and who gives us the greatest gift he could give: himself. He is the source of joy and peace, life and happiness. He is personally and purposefully at work in us for our good, every moment of every day. He will never leave us nor forsake us. He is closer than a brother, more faithful than the best of friends, more passionate about us than the greatest lover.

In this broken world, we may not always *feel* satisfied. We will always groan, and long for the full experience of satisfaction when Christ returns. But what joy to know that our deepest need has been met! What joy to know our truest desire is being satisfied! What joy to know our most noble hope and aspiration is being fulfilled! We may lack many things in this life, but we have God himself.

Prayer

Lord, you have made us for yourself,
  and our hearts are restless until they find their rest in you.
We hunger for you –
  satisfy us with your presence.
We thirst for you –
  fill us afresh with your Spirit.
Satisfy us in the morning with your unfailing love,
  that we may sing for joy and be glad all our days.
(With elements taken from Augustine and Psalm 90)

Song: *Come* **by Yvonne Lyon**

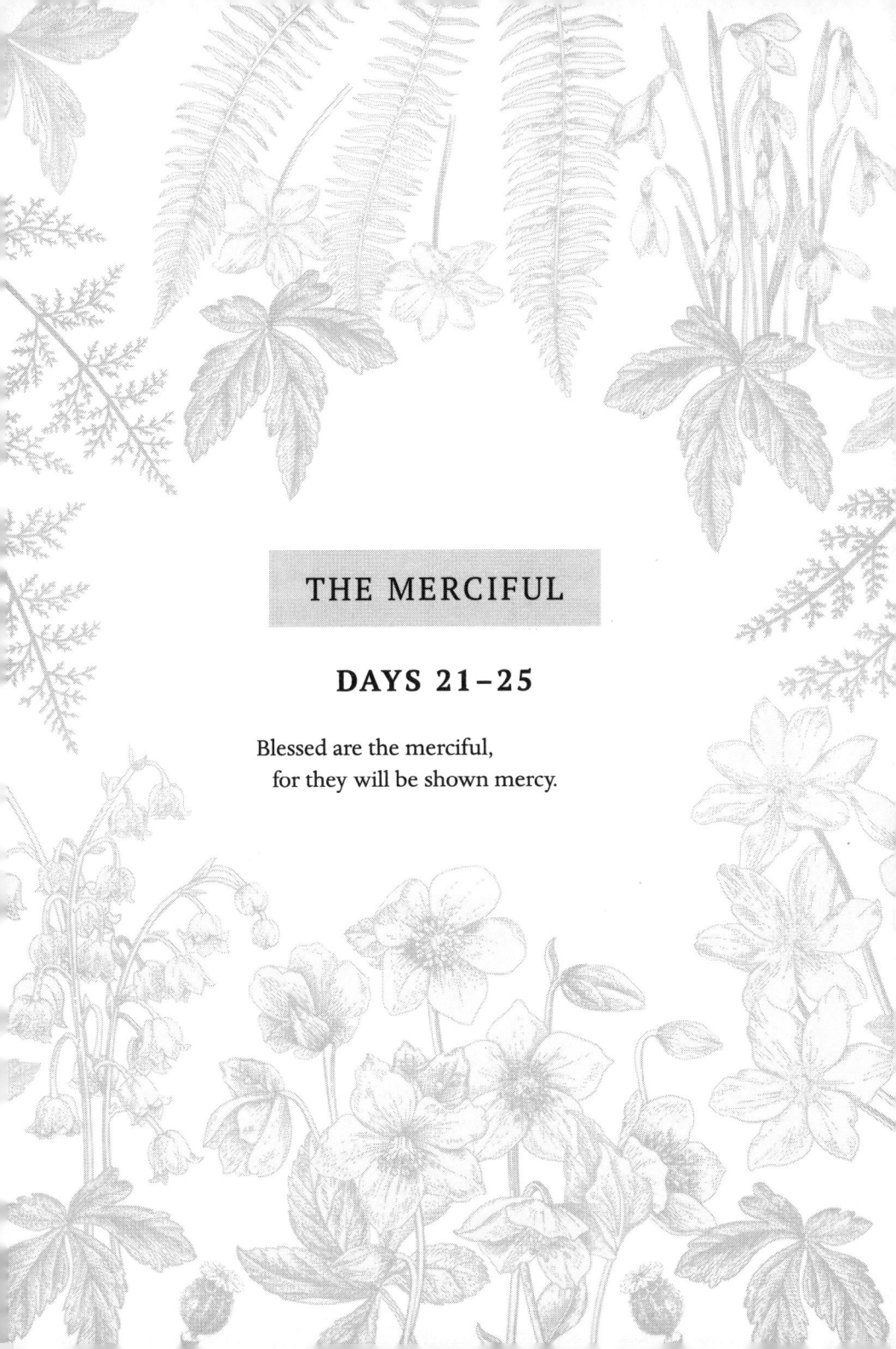

THE MERCIFUL

DAYS 21–25

Blessed are the merciful,
  for they will be shown mercy.

21

I DESIRE MERCY, NOT SACRIFICE

Blessed are the merciful,
   for they will be shown mercy.
(Matthew 5:7)

   I desire mercy, not sacrifice (Matthew 9:13 and 12:7).

This fifth beatitude is the only one where the promised 'reward' exactly matches the condition that is blessed. Jesus isn't saying that being merciful *earns* mercy from God (how could mercy be earned?!). Rather he is saying that the sure sign that we have received God's mercy is that we are merciful – kind and generous – towards others.

Once some friends of mine were expecting a Christian guest who had something of a reputation for great holiness. My friends were quite apprehensive, wondering if therefore this person would be very hard to be around. Might they need not only to tidy up their house, but also their *lives* before this person arrived? I don't know how things turned out, but this story illustrates what many of us naturally think: that to be holy is to be somewhat harsh, perhaps a little cold and even judgmental on others. Jesus' words in this fifth beatitude paint entirely the opposite picture, and his life exemplified this: true holiness means being warm-hearted.

On one occasion the pharisees were being critical of Jesus for eating with tax collectors and sinners. The pharisees were self-righteous and judgmental and unwelcoming towards others. Jesus rebuked them, quoting from Hosea: 'I desire mercy, not sacrifice' (Matthew 9:13). Mercy involves having a heart that welcomes others, not judges them.

On another occasion the pharisees criticised Jesus for letting his disciples pluck and eat grain on the sabbath. They cared more about rule-keeping than about caring for people. Again, Jesus responded with those words from Hosea: 'I desire mercy, not sacrifice' (Matthew 12:7). Mercy involves having a heart that wants to care for others, not burden them with our religious rules. This is what Christ himself is like.

Godliness is not about being cold and hard, but about being warm and generous. The holiest saints are those with the softest hearts.

For reflection

I once heard a sermon where the pastor suggested that the church have a big sign saying 'I desire mercy, not sacrifice' over its door. What do you think a church would look like that really took this principle of Jesus to heart?

What does it tell you about the character of God that he repeatedly says 'I desire mercy, not sacrifice'? Spend some time worshipping him for this now.

Prayer

> Soften my heart, Lord,
>   to be more like the heart of Jesus:
> A heart that welcomes
> That loves
> That forgives
> That honours
> That rejoices
> That comforts
> Soften my heart, Lord,
>   to be more like the heart of Jesus
> Warm my affections
>   at the fire of your love.

Song: *Blessed Are the Merciful* by The Porter's Gate

22

AS WE FORGIVE THOSE WHO SIN AGAINST US

Shouldn't you have had mercy on your fellow servant just as I had on you? (Matthew 18:33 – but read all of Matthew 18:23–35).

I wonder how you felt as you read the parable of the unmerciful servant. I think it is intended to evoke an emotional reaction. We are to feel the outrage that the servant who has been forgiven such a great debt by his master harshly refuses to forgive the much smaller debt of a fellow servant. But as always with Jesus' parables, we are drawn into the story. The master's words to the servant become Jesus' words to any Christian who refuses to forgive others: 'Shouldn't you have had mercy on your fellow servant just as I had on you?' (Matthew 18:33).

At one level, forgiveness is very simple. God has shown mercy to us, so we should be prepared to show mercy to others when they repent of their sins. But, of course, working this out in practice may be very complex. Forgiveness does *not* mean simply pretending that the offence never happened, and letting things be exactly as they were before. Calls for forgiveness should never be used to harm someone who is the victim of abuse or great wrongdoing. Jesus always calls for the weak to be protected and the wicked to be restrained and punished. Forgiveness is the refusal of *personal* vengeance and the harbouring of a bitter spirit; it is not saying that *no-one* (such as the church, the police, the state) should take action.

Even if the practical outworkings may be very complex, the heart issue is clear. As we have received mercy from God, so we should be prepared to extend mercy to others. This may feel like a hard teaching, but Jesus is laying this on us not as a burden, but as a *blessing*. Forgiveness is one of the great blessings of the Christian life: not simply that we are forgiven by God, but also that by his grace we are enabled to forgive others. We have a Father who cares for us deeply, we have a God who will make sure justice is ultimately done, and so we can be freed from crippling bitterness. God's heart is by nature merciful – and by his grace he enables us to grow more like him and have merciful hearts ourselves.

Prayer

O merciful God,
   fill our hearts with the graces of your Holy Spirit,
with love, joy, peace,
   patience, gentleness, goodness,
   faith, meekness, and self-control.
Teach us to love those who hate us,
   to pray for those who spite us,
that we may be called children of you, our Father,
   who makes your sun to shine on the evil and on the good,
   and sends rain on the just and on the unjust.
In adversity grant us grace to be patient;
   in prosperity keep us humble;
may we guard the door of our lips;
may we lightly esteem the pleasures of this world,
   and thirst after heavenly things;
through Jesus Christ our Lord. Amen.
– **Anselm**

Song: *Beatitude* **by Yaz Williams**

23

THE ONE WHO HAD MERCY ON HIM

'Which of these three do you think was a neighbour to the man who fell into the hands of robbers?' The expert in the law replied, 'The one who had mercy on him.' Jesus told him, 'Go and do likewise' (Luke 10:36–37 – but read the whole story).

One of the most beautiful scriptural pictures of 'showing mercy' – in its broadest sense – is the story of the good Samaritan. It is an emotional tale of great suffering and then great kindness, as well as no little surprise: the hero is not one of the religious 'good guys' but rather a despised Samaritan.

This story sets out in concrete and vivid form what it means to 'show mercy'. The Samaritan's mercy is not a begrudging mercy: he first has compassion on the man. He is moved by his suffering. Mercy begins in the heart. But then the Samaritan *acts*: he moves towards the man, where so many others moved away. Getting involved with this man took time and energy. It cost money. It might involve getting ceremonially unclean. For the priest and the Levite it was just too costly. But the Samaritan approached and tenderly bound up the man's wounds. This man's suffering wasn't an embarrassment to him. Helping the man wasn't beneath him – even though, as a Samaritan, normally he would have had nothing to do with a Jew.

The Samaritan bore a considerable cost to care for the man. He put the man on his own donkey (so he himself would have to walk). Then he gave money to the innkeeper to look after the man, as well as promising to come back and pay anything else that was needed.

We can't help but see a picture of our God's mercy to us in this story. A heart of compassion. Moving towards our suffering. Tender personal care. Paying a great cost himself to secure not just our present, but our future. And all while we were his enemies. In this story we see a picture of our situation, and a wonderfully moving picture of the Lord's mercy towards us. Surely the right response is to marvel and worship at the mercy of our God!

But as we marvel at God's mercy – his kind, compassionate and costly mercy – we then hear Jesus' call to share in his wonderful character: 'Go and do likewise' (Luke 10:37).

Prayer

Father, thank you for the comfort we know in Christ
  and our fellowship in the Spirit
Thank you for Jesus
  who set aside his riches
  who laid down his rights
  and who poured himself out to death for us
May I never think of myself more highly than I ought
  but see myself as a servant of Christ
May I not look to my own interests
  but seek the interests of others
Guard me from selfish ambition and conceit
  and grant me a quiet and humble spirit
For such is the blessed way of Christ
  and in such things you delight, O Lord.
(**Adapted from Philippians 2:1–11**)

Song: *Holy Water* by **We The Kingdom, Tasha Cobbs Leonard**

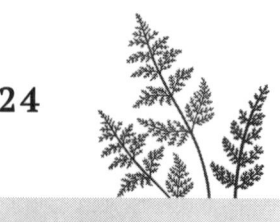

24

MERCY TO THE POOR

He who despises his neighbour sins;
But he who has mercy on the poor, happy *is* he.
(**Proverbs 14:21** NKJV)

In Jesus' day, 'showing mercy' would have included not just forgiving those who sin against us, but also being generous to the poor and needy. The word Jesus uses for 'mercy' is used in Proverbs 14:21 to speak of practical care for the poor.

Lent has traditionally been a particular time for remembering the poor and needy in our churches and communities. It may be donating money or goods. It may be giving time to serve those who are needy in various ways. Sometimes it may be partnered with fasting: we give up something (luxuries, money, time) in order to be able to share that with those in need.

Generosity to those who are poor or afflicted is a mark of a heart that has been conformed to that of Christ: 'For you know the grace of our Lord Jesus Christ, that though he was rich, yet for your sake he became poor, so that you through his poverty might become rich' (2 Corinthians 8:9).

Care for the poor and needy within the church is one of the ways we can express our love for Christ himself: 'Truly I tell you, whatever you did for one of the least of these brothers and sisters of mine, you did for me' (Matthew 25:40).

Paul even goes as far as to say the reason that we have been blessed so much is so that we can be generous with it:

> And God is able to bless you abundantly, *so that* in all things at all times, having all that you need, you will abound in every good work ... You will be enriched in every way *so that* you can be generous on every occasion (2 Corinthians 9:8,11, emphasis added).

Care for those in need should always be part of our life as Christian disciples, but Lent can be a particular opportunity to grow in this practice, or rekindle it. It is part of the paradoxical way of discipleship. The way down is the way up. It is more blessed to give than to receive.

Reflection

Perhaps you might talk and pray about the following questions in your family, household or community group:

- Who are those in need in your church / community?
- What might it look like in practice to show mercy to them?

Prayer

> Lord Jesus Christ, we love you!
> Thank you that we can express this love
>   as we care for the needs of your people.
> When we see you hungry
>   may we give you something to eat,
> When we see you thirsty
>   may we give you something to drink,
> When we see you in the face of stranger
>   may we invite you in,
> When you need clothes
>   may we clothe you,
> When you are sick
>   may we look after you,
> When you are in prison
>   may we come to visit you,
> Lord Jesus Christ, we love you!
> Help us to express this love
>   as we care for the needs of your people.
> Amen.

Song: *Let Us Be Known* by The Porter's Gate and Diana Gameros

(this song begins in Spanish, then switches to English)

25

A MERCY-SHAPED HEART

We've seen that mercy is about more than just forgiveness, it is about more than just good deeds towards others (though it does include those things). Being merciful means having a beautiful God-shaped heart of kindness and generosity to those in need.

To close our reflections on mercy, we'll use some words adapted from 1 Corinthians 13. These originally spoke about love, but apply equally to the closely related virtue of mercy.

You may wish to read these words slowly and prayerfully, and do so a couple of times. The first time, perhaps reflect on God's amazing merciful heart towards us. Then read them again, asking for God's help to grow in this beautiful grace of mercy.

A merciful heart is patient and kind.
A merciful heart does not envy,
   does not boast, is not proud.
A merciful heart does not dishonour others
   (instead, it seeks out ways to honour them).
A merciful heart is not self-seeking
   (instead, it seeks the good of others).
A merciful heart is not easily angered
   and keeps no record of wrongs.
A merciful heart does not delight in evil
   but rejoices with the truth.
A merciful heart always protects
   and always trusts.
A merciful heart always hopes
   and always perseveres.
(Adapted from 1 Corinthians 13)

Prayer

Lord, make me an instrument of your peace;
Where hate rules, let me bring love,
Where malice, forgiveness,
Where disputes, reconciliation,
Where error, truth,
Where doubt, belief,
Where despair, hope,
Where darkness, Thy light,
Where sorrow, joy!

O Master, let me strive more to comfort others than to be
comforted,
To understand others than to be understood,
To love others, more than to be loved!

For he who gives, receives,
He who forgets himself, finds,
He who forgives, receives forgiveness,
And dying, we rise again to eternal life. Amen.
– Francis of Assisi

Song: *Thy Mercy, My God* **by Sandra McCracken**

SEEING GOD

DAYS 26–30

Blessed are the pure in heart,
for they will see God.

26

THEY WILL SEE GOD

Blessed are the pure in heart,
  for they will see God.
(**Matthew 5:8**)

For this beatitude we're going to take a different approach of first considering the second half: 'they will see God'. If we understand not just what this second half means, but why it is so important – and wonderful – we will be better placed to consider the first part about purity of heart.

The whole Bible consistently presents God himself as our greatest joy and delight. The chief glory of the new heavens and the new earth will not so much be the city with gates of gold, the renewed and glorious creation, or even the fact that we will finally be free from suffering, sin and all that we struggle with here and now. The chief glory of the new creation will be our God himself. As the old hymn puts it: 'The lamb is all the glory of Immanuel's land.'³

Not only is God the chief joy of the new creation, but knowing him is the greatest joy of this life now. Eternal life *is* knowing the one true God and Jesus Christ whom he sent (John 17:3). Eternal life has begun *now* for those who are in Christ. Christ truly is our hope in life and death.

One day, those who have been purified by Christ will enter our eternal bliss and see our Saviour face to face. But even now, we can 'see God' – not a literal seeing, but a growing knowledge of him, a deepening relational intimacy with him. Like David, we can 'gaze on the beauty of the LORD' (Psalm 27:4).

Do you want joy and fruitfulness in life? Gaze on Christ. Do you want comfort in afflictions, and hope for the future? Gaze on Christ. Do you want life to the full, do you want to be the best version of yourself that you can be? Gaze on Christ. He sweetens every joy, he tempers every sorrow; he strengthens every good work, he lightens every gloom. He is light, he is love, he is justice, he is goodness, he is beauty. Gaze on him.

Prayer

Eternal God, eternal Trinity,
You have made the Blood of Christ so precious
　through His sharing in Your Divine nature.
You are a mystery as deep as the sea;
　the more I search, the more I find,
　and the more I find, the more I search for You.
But I can never be satisfied;
　what I receive will ever leave me desiring more.
When You fill my soul, I have an ever-greater hunger,
　and I grow more famished for Your light.
I desire above all to see You,
　the true light, as you really are. Amen.
– **Catherine of Siena**

Song: *Woke Up This Morning* by Tamesha Pruett-Ray

27

TO SEE CHRIST'S GLORY

Father, I want those you have given me to be with me where I am,
and to see my glory (John 17:24).

For today's devotion, we will continue to think on the extraordinary
privilege of gazing on Christ. We will use words from the first chapter of
John Owen's book *The Glory of Christ*. Some of these quotes are quite dense,
so you may wish just to choose one or two to meditate on slowly, as they
repay taking time with them.

> The greatest desire that Christ expressed in his prayer was that his
> people might be with him to behold his glory (John 17:24). The Lord
> Christ desired that his disciples should see his glory in order that they
> might be filled with joy and happiness for evermore.

> Only a sight of his glory, and nothing else, will truly satisfy God's
> people. The hearts of believers are like a magnetized needle which
> cannot rest until it is pointing north. So also, a believer, magnetized
> by the love of Christ, will always be restless until he or she comes to
> Christ and beholds his glory.

> One of the greatest privileges the believer has, both in this world
> and for eternity, is to behold the glory of Christ. On this depend our
> present comforts and future blessedness. This is the life and reward
> of our souls (John 14:9; 2 Corinthians 4:6).

> It is only as we behold the glory of Christ by faith here in this world
> that our hearts will be drawn more and more to Christ and to the full
> enjoyment of the sight of his glory hereafter.

In Christ's face we shall see the glory of God in his infinite perfections. These things will shine into our souls filling us for ever with peace, rest, and glory.

By beholding the glory of Christ by faith we shall find rest to our souls. Our minds are apt to be filled with troubles, fears, cares, dangers, distresses, ungoverned passions and lusts. By these our thoughts are filled with chaos, darkness and confusion. But where the soul is fixed on the glory of Christ, then the mind finds rest and peace for 'to be spiritually minded is peace' (Romans 8:6).

By beholding the glory of Christ, we shall begin to experience what it means to be everlastingly blessed. 'We shall always be with the Lord' (1 Thessalonians 4:17). We shall 'be with Christ,' which is best of all (Philippians 1:23). For there we shall 'behold his glory' (John 17:24). And by seeing him as he is, 'we shall be made like him' (1 John 3:2). This is our everlasting blessedness.

Prayer

O God, our refuge, it is good to be near you –
  who do we have in heaven but you?
  There is nothing to be desired more than you.
Be with us continually today –
  hold our right hand
  guide us with your counsel
  and afterwards receive us to glory.
Though our heart and flesh may fail,
  be the strength of our heart
  and our portion for ever.
(Adapted from Psalm 73)

Song: *Christ Our Hope in Life and Death* by Steph Macleod and Sandra McCracken

28

CLEAN WINDOWS

Blessed are the pure in heart,
   for they will see God.
(Matthew 5:8)

We now turn to the first part of the beatitude. The astonishing privilege of seeing God belongs only to the pure in heart. This is true of the new creation: our hearts will be perfectly pure and we will see God face to face. But is also true *now*. As we pursue purity, we are enabled to see God better. We can *increasingly* gaze on his beauty, deepening in knowledge of him and relationship with him. In this beatitude, Jesus says that our ability to see God in this life will be dependent on the purity of our hearts.

One year, my family went up to the Keswick Convention in the Lake District, and we stayed in a cottage that had a beautiful view down the valley. Each day, it was a joy to gaze out of the window and see the countryside changing in the different weather and light. It was truly stunning. Imagine now if the owners of the cottage had never cleaned the windows. Imagine if, over time, grime and dirt built up so that eventually the glorious view was completely obscured.

This is a picture of what sin does. It prevents us from seeing the beauty of our Lord. It is like the grime on the windows of our lives. The more we dabble in sin, the dimmer the light of God's glory seems, the less clear and distinctly we can see him. Maybe we don't often think of sin this way. We think of the guilt of sin, but often forget the 'grime' of sin and how it spoils our view of God.

If we want to know God, if we want to experience his goodness, we must pursue holiness. We don't do so alone. The Holy Spirit has been described as having a 'spotlight' ministry, shining light on Christ so he may be seen better. Maybe we also need to think of the 'window-cleaning' ministry of the Spirit. As he helps us to fight sin and pursue purity, he is enabling us to see Christ more clearly. Purity is not a burdensome duty, but an invitation to the *infinite* good of knowing God better. It is an invitation to heaven itself.

Prayer

O wonderful and mighty God,
  whose power and wisdom have no end,
before whom all powers tremble,
  and at whose glance the heavens and the earth flee away,
You are Love, you are my Father,
  and I will love and worship you for ever and ever!
You have shown pity on me,
  and a ray from your light has shone upon my inward eye.
Guide me on into the perfect light,
  that it may illumine me wholly,
  and that all darkness may flee away.
Let the holy flame of your love so burn in my heart
  that it be made pure, and I may see you, O God;
  for it is the pure in heart who see you.
You have set me free; You have drawn me to yourself;
  therefore do not forsake me,
  but keep me always in your grace.
Guide me, and rule me,
  and perfect me for your kingdom. Amen.

– **Augustine**

Song: *Open the Eyes of My Heart* by **Audrey Assad**

29

GUARD YOUR HEART

Above all else, guard your heart,
  for everything you do flows from it.
(**Proverbs 4:23**)

If we read on beyond the beatitudes in the sermon on the mount, it becomes very clear that Jesus cares about our hearts. He desires more than just outward conformity to a set of laws ('you shall not murder', 'you shall not commit adultery'); he is concerned with what is going on in our hearts.

It's easy to think of sin just in relation to guilt and punishment. And so perhaps we think that, if Christ has paid the debt for our sins and if we can 'get away with it' in this life, then a little sin doesn't have much impact on us. But we need to think about the impact on our hearts. We are creatures of habit. The more we engage in particular thoughts or actions (whether good or bad), the more ingrained these will become.

Imagine sledging down a hill on a snowy day. The first time you do so, with the snow all pristine before you, you have complete freedom of where to turn. But if you sledge down the same route multiple times, the snow will become compressed, and the sledge will naturally follow the same path each time, with more and more effort required to move off it.

So it is with our hearts. We are creatures of habit. The more we follow certain paths, the easier it becomes to do so. Certain actions or thoughts become second nature to us. And it can take time to change these. This is why the writer of Proverbs encourages us to guard our hearts. Everything else flows from there. If we have a heart full of anger, greed, lust or ambition, eventually this will work its way out in our actions. Character matters.

Gloriously, we are not on our own as we seek to guard our hearts. We do so safe in the arms of a Father who loves us. We do so in the power of God's Holy Spirit living within us, helping us with all Christ's strength. And we labour for purity knowing the infinite blessings that this leads to: an increasing vision of the goodness and glory of our Saviour Jesus Christ!

Reflection

Are there patterns of thought or action that are not helpful to your heart, that you would like Christ's help to change?

Are there patterns of thought or action that might prove helpful to you, and you would like Christ's help to grow in?

Prayer

> Father, by your Spirit, help me to fight sin in my heart
>> that I may have eyes to see the beauty of Christ
>
> Keep me from pride
>> that I may see Christ's beauty
>
> Keep me from greed
>> that I may see Christ's beauty
>
> Keep me from lust
>> that I may see Christ's beauty
>
> Keep me from envy
>> that I may see Christ's beauty
>
> Keep me from gluttony
>> that I may see Christ's beauty
>
> Keep me from wrath
>> that I may see Christ's beauty
>
> Keep me from sloth
>> that I may see Christ's beauty
>
> Jesus, I want to see you.

Song: *Canticle* by TAYA, Jon Guerra

30

BEHOLDING AND BECOMING

And we all, who with unveiled faces contemplate the Lord's glory, are being transformed into his image with ever-increasing glory, which comes from the Lord, who is the Spirit (2 Corinthians 3:18).

We've seen that one of the great reasons for pursuing holiness is that it will increase our capacity to drink in the glory and beauty of our Saviour. As we grow in purity of heart, we grow in vision of God. There is nothing more worthwhile that we could pursue, in this life or in the one to come.

Today's verse shows us the virtuous circle that there is in seeing God. Purity of heart enables us to see more of God, and the reverse is also true. Contemplating Christ's glory is itself transformative, and is part of how God conforms us to the likeness of Christ. The more we behold him, the more we become like him. The more we become like him, the more we are able to see him as he truly is. This will be the glorious pattern for all eternity, as we are enfolded in the loving embrace of our Father, Son and Holy Spirit!

Part of pursuing purity of heart, therefore, involves taking the attention *off* ourselves! There is a right place for self-examination, and Lent is a particular season for this. But this is only ever a means to a greater end: gazing on our Saviour. If you want your heart to be set on fire with love for Christ, don't look within and seek to kindle your own fires; rather look up to Christ and the white-hot glory of his goodness and grace!

Scottish pastor M'Cheyne put this beautifully:

> For every look at yourself, take ten looks at Christ. He is altogether lovely. Such infinite majesty, and yet such meekness and grace, and all for sinners, even the chief! Live much in the smiles of God. Bask in his beams. Feel his all-seeing eye settled on you in love, and repose in his almighty arms … Let your soul be filled with a heart-ravishing sense of the sweetness and excellency of Christ and all that is in him. Let the Holy Spirit fill every chamber of your heart; and so there will be no room for folly, or the world, or Satan, or the flesh.[4]

Prayer

O my sweet Lord Jesus,
  pierce my inmost soul
with the most joyous and healthful wound of your love,
  that it may melt with love and longing for you,
let my soul hunger alone for you:
  the bread of life:
let it thirst after you,
  the spring and fountain of eternal light,
  the stream of true pleasure;
May I always desire you, seek you, and find you,
  and sweetly rest in you. Amen.

– **Bonaventura (lightly edited)**

Song: *Fairest Lord Jesus* **by Sara Groves**

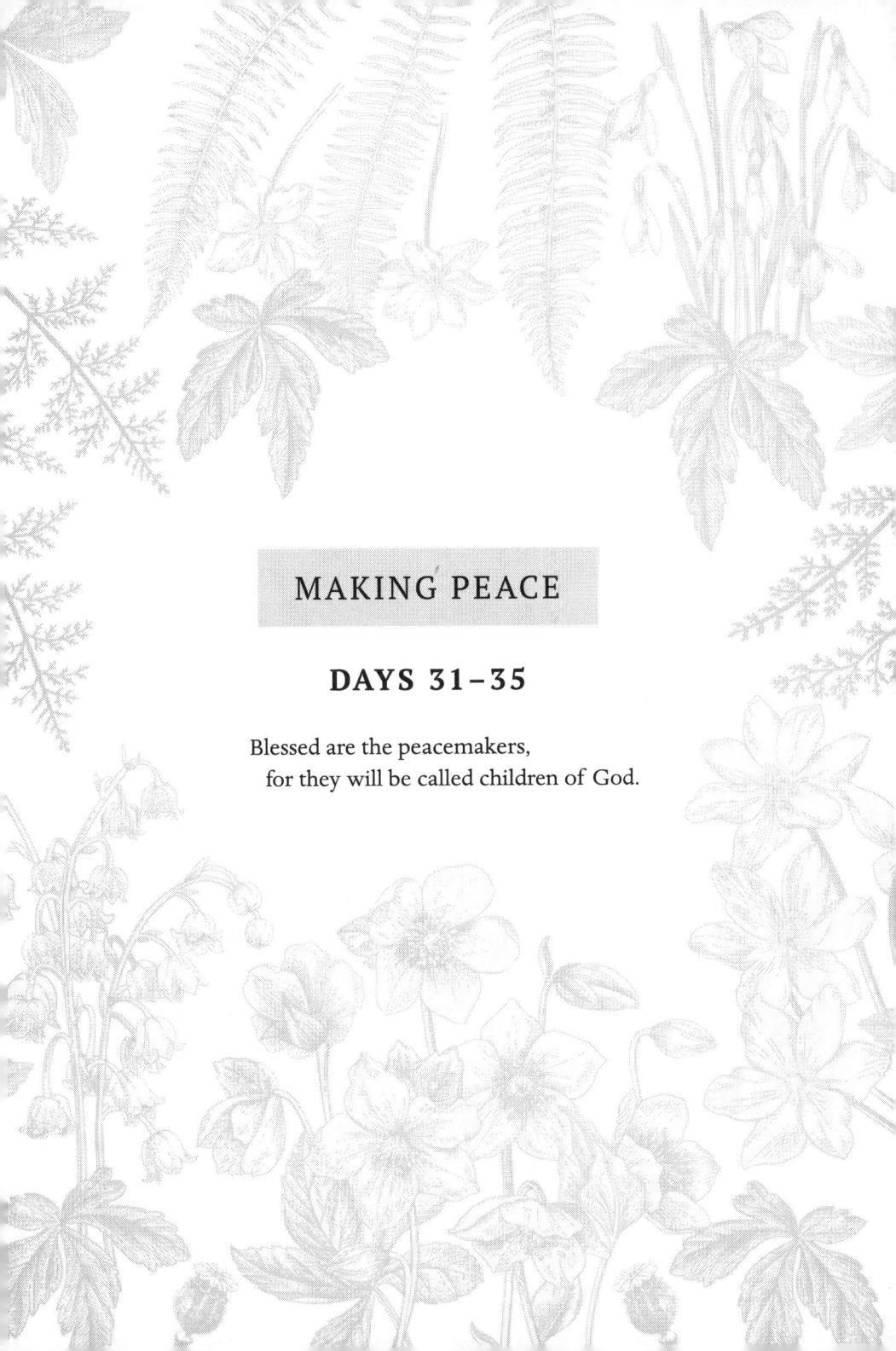

MAKING PEACE

DAYS 31–35

Blessed are the peacemakers,
  for they will be called children of God.

31

PRINCE OF PEACE

Blessed are the peacemakers,
  for they will be called children of God.
(**Matthew 5:9**)

And he will be called
  Wonderful Counsellor, Mighty God,
  Everlasting Father, Prince of Peace.
(**Isaiah 9:6**)

Peace is a hugely significant Bible word. In the Old Testament the word for peace is 'shalom', which means far more than absence of conflict. It also signifies completeness, wholeness, things being as they should be. When Isaiah calls Jesus 'Prince of Peace', he is saying that Jesus is the one who will restore all things. First and foremost, Christ restores our broken relationship with God: by paying for our sins, he brings us peace with God (Romans 5:1).

The wonderful, good news is that, no matter how we feel, if we are Christians, we *have* peace with God. Jesus has paid for our sins and has reconciled us to God. We could not be closer to God than we already are. In fact, since we are united to Christ, we are as close to God as Jesus the Son is to his Father. There is *no* condemnation for those who are in Christ Jesus. And there is no *separation* either. The sins that might drive us away have all been dealt with. We have peace with God. We rest in his warm loving embrace!

Our broken relationship with God led to every other pain and conflict in the world. And so Jesus bringing us peace with God paves the way for everything else then to be put right. Right relationships with others, and a right relationship with the world – a return to the paradise of Eden!

Before we think about how we are called to be peacemakers, let's think first on God, *the* peacemaker. This Easter, as we look ahead to Jesus' death on the cross, let's remember why he walked this path. Let's remember that peace we have with God. Let's remember the peace – the *shalom* – that he brings to the world.

Reflection and prayer

The following passages from Isaiah add more colour to the picture of the peace Jesus brings. You may wish to choose one or more to meditate on, then spend some time in thanks and adoration.

> The LORD will surely comfort Zion
> and will look with compassion on all her ruins;
> he will make her deserts like Eden,
> her wastelands like the garden of the LORD.
> Joy and gladness will be found in her,
> thanksgiving and the sound of singing. (Isaiah 51:3)

> How beautiful on the mountains
> are the feet of those who bring good news, who proclaim peace,
> who bring good tidings, who proclaim salvation,
> who say to Zion, 'Your God reigns!'
> Listen! Your watchmen lift up their voices;
> together they shout for joy.
> When the LORD returns to Zion, they will see it with their own eyes.
> Burst into songs of joy together, you ruins of Jerusalem,
> for the LORD has comforted his people,
> he has redeemed Jerusalem. (Isaiah 52:7–9)

> 'Though the mountains be shaken and the hills be removed,
> yet my unfailing love for you will not be shaken
> nor my covenant of peace be removed,'
> says the LORD, who has compassion on you.
> 'Afflicted city, lashed by storms and not comforted,
> I will rebuild you with stones of turquoise,
> your foundations with lapis lazuli.
> I will make your battlements of rubies, your gates of sparkling jewels,
> and all your walls of precious stones.
> All your children will be taught by the LORD,
> and great will be their peace.' (Isaiah 54:10–13)

Song: *Shalom* by Bridge Worship, Setnick Sene

32

UNITY IN THE CHURCH

How good and pleasant it is
   when God's people live together in unity!
   (**Psalm 133:1**)

In a world so badly fractured and broken, how wonderful that Christ's church is called to be so different. The church is to be a place of unity. This was seen in the early church by the two great religious groups – Jews and Gentiles, who would have normally been hostile to each other – being brought to unity and fellowship by Christ.

In one sense, then, peace in the church is not something that we have to labour to achieve. We have been united in Christ. But what we are called to do is to *live out* that unity. We are to *maintain* the unity of the spirit through the bond of peace (Ephesians 4:3).

Psalm 133 celebrates the blessing of when God's people live together in unity. When churches are healthy, they are places of welcome, of unity, of peace. A united church is a blessing to those who are part of it, and a beacon of light in a dark world. True unity – unity in diversity – is a glorious Christian distinctive.

Living out the unity we have in Christ will take effort, as our sinful nature will always tend to disunity. But living Christ's way is not only beautiful and desirable; it is possible by his spirit.

We are often quick to divide, yet Christ calls us to be one. We are often quick to seek our own way, but Christ tells us to prefer others. We are often quick to take offence, yet Christ calls us to bear with others. We are often quick to speak, but Christ calls us to be quick to listen. We are often quick to think the best of ourselves, but Christ tells us to think the best of others. We are often quick to favour those who are like us, but Christ calls us to pay particular attention to those who are *unlike* us. We are often quick to criticise others, but Christ tells us to honour them.

Christ died not just to reconcile us to God, but to reconcile us to each other. What a beautiful and wonderful thing this is! What Christ has joined together, let no-one separate.

Prayer

Holy Spirit,
Comforting fire, Life of all creation.
Anointing the sick, cleansing body and soul,
Fill this body!

Holy Spirit,
Sacred breath, Fire of love,
Sweetest taste, Beautiful aroma,
Fill this heart!

Holy Spirit,
Filling the world, from the heights to the deep,
Raining from clouds, filling rivers and sea,
Fill this mind!

Holy Spirit,
Forgiving and giving,
uniting strangers, reconciling enemies,
Seeking the lost, and enfolding us together,
Fill these gathered here!

Holy Spirit,
Bringing light into dark places, igniting praise,
Greatest gift, our Hope and Encourager,
Holy Spirit of Christ,
I praise you! Amen.
– **Hildegard of Bingen**

Song: *Siyahamba / We Are Marching* **by The Ethnos Project**

NO FAVOURITISM

My brothers and sisters, believers in our glorious Lord Jesus Christ
must not show favouritism (James 2:1 – but read all of James 2:1–9).

The church is to be a place of peace. As Christians, we have peace with
God, through the work of Christ, and this is to be expressed in peace with
one another. No one group is to be prioritised above another. Favouritism has
no place in God's new society. This was one of the shining distinctives of the
early church.

Tragically, as humans we are always prone to divide into different groups,
into 'those who are like us' and 'those who are different', or 'those who are
with us' and 'those who are against us'. We see such divisions due to ethnicity,
social background, gender, physical or mental 'ability', and so many more.
We are prone to show favouritism, whether this is done intentionally or not.
Favouritism is a sin we can commit 'through ignorance, through weakness, or
through our own deliberate fault' – yet whichever of these it is, it is still a sin.

Yet to the church, Jesus would say 'not so with you'. We have been brought
into one family, and so we should live as such. How can I look down on a
brother for whom Christ died? How can I exclude a sister who is precious
in Christ's eyes? How can I turn away from or ignore a particular group of
people, knowing that I will spend eternity with them in glory? These things
are easy to say, but I know in my own heart how hard they can be to live
out. My old prejudices die hard. My ignorance and privilege blind me to the
experience of those who are on the margins.

But peacemakers – those who seek to combat the favouritism in their own
hearts and in the church – are those who will be called children of God: a
Hebrew image meaning being *like* God. God's heart beats with peace. God
went to extraordinary lengths to unite humanity to him, and unite us to each
other. When we seek peace, even when it is hard and costly, we are living the
blessed life, because we are sharing in our Father's wonderful likeness.

Reflection

Commenting on James 2:1, Trillia Newbell asks these penetrating questions:[5]

- Could it be that you are partial to those who are just like you?
- Could it be partiality that hinders your own pursuit of diversity?

One further question I'm trying to ask myself is this:

- Might someone feel excluded by me or the group that I am part of (whether intentionally or not) on the basis of:
  - ~ gender?
  - ~ age?
  - ~ skin colour?
  - ~ social background?
  - ~ how 'useful' we think someone is to church?
  - ~ theological viewpoint?
  - ~ social skills?
  - ~ something else?

Why not talk to God about some of these things now.

Prayer

> O God of endurance and encouragement,
> Grant us to live in such harmony with one another
>   In accord with Christ Jesus
> That, together with one voice,
>   we may glorify the God and Father of our Lord Jesus Christ.
> **(Based on Romans 15:5)**

Song: *Kyrie Eleison* by Keith and Kristyn Getty

34

PURSUING PEACE

Jesus calls his disciples to be 'peace*makers*'. That is, we are not simply to avoid behaviour that will cause hurt, division and oppression. We are to *pursue* peace; we are to be active in seeking to make our churches and our societies places of peace, of wholeness, of shalom. There is effort involved; it may be costly. But this is the path that God's children are called to walk, following the example of our heavenly Father.

The Bible has a rich picture of what this will look like in practice. Today's devotion gives an opportunity to reflect on some of the Bible's main passages on peace. You may choose to read all the passages, or just spend time with one. If it is helpful, you may wish to make notes in the table below, or you may prefer just to choose a passage to meditate on slowly.

What does this tell me about peacemaking?	What might this look like in practice for me / my church?	How did Jesus perfectly exemplify this?

If it is possible, as far as it depends on you, live at peace with everyone (Romans 12:18).

Deceit is in the hearts of those who plot evil,
  but those who promote peace have joy.
(**Proverbs 12:20**)

The wisdom that comes from heaven is first of all pure; then peace-
loving, considerate, submissive, full of mercy and good fruit,
impartial and sincere. Peacemakers who sow in peace reap a harvest
of righteousness (James 3:17–18).

Whoever would love life
  and see good days
must keep their tongue from evil
  and their lips from deceitful speech.
They must turn from evil and do good;
  they must seek peace and pursue it.
For the eyes of the Lord are on the righteous
  and his ears are attentive to their prayer,
but the face of the Lord is against those who do evil.
(**1 Peter 3:10–12, quoting Psalm 34**)

Prayer

Heavenly Father,
You have welcomed us in Christ
  and united us to each other
Help us, by your Holy Spirit,
  to love each other deeply
  to offer hospitality without grumbling
  and to use our gifts to serve others
doing all in the strength you provide
  and for your glory. Amen.
(**Adapted from 1 Peter 4**)

Song: *An Instrument of Peace* **by The Porter's Gate**

35

PEACE ON EARTH

Glory to God in the highest heaven,
   and on earth peace to those on whom his favour rests.
(**Luke 2:14**)

'Peace on earth' is a phrase that perhaps seems tired or trite, sounding like the words of a beauty pageant contestant, or a politician seeking votes. Yet this was the message of the angels on the hillside above Bethlehem as they announced the birth of Jesus. Jesus was coming to bring peace: the *shalom* that is more than just absence of conflict, but includes wholeness, completeness, prosperity and fruitfulness.

This will only be completely fulfilled in the new creation, when humanity lives in perfect peace with God, but it doesn't stop God caring about peace now. God is making a new world, but he still wants his will to be done on *earth* as it is in heaven. Heavenly-minded Christians are called to be good earthly citizens (Romans 12 and 13). Christians, therefore, should care about peace on earth.

In her insightful book on the beatitudes, Rebekah Eklund notes both how hard and how important it is to be a peacemaker:

> Sustained reflection on how to make peace through just means is urgently needed today. More and more, peacemakers must consider not only how to make peace but how to create the conditions that make violence less likely, and how to rebuild societies when violence leaves such a wide swath of destruction in its wake, crippling transportation, health systems, and education. The world needs more peacemakers.[6]

One vital part of being a peacemaker will be spreading the good news of Jesus. Only through Jesus can people be reconciled to God and know peace with him – the deepest and most significant peace of all. And as we are reconciled to God, this overflows into reconciliation with one another. So, if we desire peace on earth – as we should – this should drive us out into the world with the good news of Jesus, the prince of peace!

Blessed are the peacemakers, for they will be called sons of God. Blessed are the peacemakers, for they are living like *the* Son of God.

Reflection

Are there ways you could be seeking to make peace (or make the conditions in which peace may flourish) in your community?

Could you pray for opportunities to share the good news of Jesus, the prince of peace, longing that through him those around you might come to know peace with God?

Prayer

O God, who is Peace everlasting,
   whose chosen reward is the gift of peace,
   and who has taught us that the peacemakers are your children,
pour your peace into our souls,
   that everything discordant may utterly vanish,
and all that makes for peace be sweet to us for ever;
   through Jesus Christ our Lord. Amen.
– **Mozarabic liturgy**

Song: *Citizens* **by Jon Guerra**

PERSECUTED BECAUSE OF RIGHTEOUSNESS

DAYS 36–40

Blessed are those who are persecuted because
of righteousness,
for theirs is the kingdom of heaven.

36

BECAUSE OF RIGHTEOUSNESS

Blessed are those who are persecuted because of righteousness,
   for theirs is the kingdom of heaven.
(Matthew 5:10)

In the flow of the beatitudes so far, the final beatitude may come as
something of a surprise. What has been portrayed is a *beautiful* life. Just
imagine a society where people lived out this teaching. Where people were
poor in spirit, exhibiting true and vital dependence on God. Where people
mourned both their sin and the injustices in society. Where people were
meek and humble, not hungering for self-advancement, but hungering and
thirsting for righteousness. Where they were merciful towards others, pure
in heart, and sought to build bridges and make peace. This is a picture of true
righteousness. This is a picture of heaven.

But the final beatitude shows that living according to the first seven
beatitudes will often lead to persecution. And yet Jesus says that this is *still*
the blessed life. What may be something of a surprise in the flow of the
beatitudes (that this beautiful righteous life leads to persecution) should not
be a surprise as we consider the example of our Saviour. He perfectly lived
out the first seven beatitudes. He lived a glorious, godly, selfless life. And yet
he suffered for it.

For this final set of devotions, we're going to take a different approach to the
rest. We're going to focus on the *one* who was persecuted for righteousness.
In this week before Easter, we're going to focus on Jesus' death. Over the next
four days, we'll focus on events from the corresponding day in Holy week. But
for today, let's survey the whole of Jesus' journey to the cross. Let's ponder
how each event happened because Jesus was *righteous*. It was Jesus' goodness
that led him to walk this path, and it was his goodness that led people to do
these things to him. And let's praise and adore him for it.

Reflection and prayer

Here are 14 moments in the account of Jesus' death, mostly drawn from Mark's gospel, but with additions from other gospels. For each of these, you may wish to:

- Picture the scene
- Meditate on what this meant for Jesus
- Meditate on what this means for your life
- Pray a short prayer of adoration

1. Jesus prays in the Garden of Gethsemane (Mark 14:32–42)
2. Jesus is betrayed by Judas and arrested (Mark 14:43–52)
3. Jesus comes before the Sanhedrin and false witnesses (Mark 14:53–65)
4. Jesus is denied by Peter three times (Mark 14:66–72)
5. Jesus is condemned to death and Barabbas set free (Mark 15:1–15)
6. Jesus is scourged and crowned with thorns (Mark 15:16–20)
7. Jesus is led to the place of the skull and crucified (Mark 15:21–27)
8. Jesus is mocked while on the cross (Mark 15:28–32)
9. Jesus promises paradise to the penitent criminal (Luke 23:39–43)
10. Jesus cries, 'My God, why have you forsaken me?' (Mark 15:33–35)
11. Jesus cries, 'It is finished.' (John 19:30)
12. Jesus dies on the cross, and the temple curtain is torn in two (Mark 15:36–41)
13. Jesus' side is pierced with a spear, but no bones are broken (John 19:33–34)
14. Jesus is laid in the tomb (Mark 15:42–47)

Song: *Were You There?* by Red Mountain Music

37

THIRTY PIECES OF SILVER (WEDNESDAY)

Then one of the Twelve – the one called Judas Iscariot – went to the chief priests and asked, 'What are you willing to give me if I deliver him over to you?' So they counted out for him thirty pieces of silver. From then on Judas watched for an opportunity to hand him over (Matthew 26:14–16).

We don't know exactly when Judas betrayed Jesus, but traditionally it is assumed to have been on the Wednesday of Holy Week. He did so for 30 pieces of silver: the amount a slave was worth (Exodus 21:32), which shows the little value Judas put on Jesus.

This story of betrayal is so familiar that we can quickly gloss over it, but it is worth taking time over. Facing opposition and persecution is painful at all times, but the pain is only magnified when it is a close friend's doing.

Jesus had lived with Judas for three years. He had *loved* Judas for three years. He had eaten meals with him; he had walked and talked with him. Jesus had opened up to him, and made himself vulnerable. All the while, Jesus would have known that Judas was going to deliver him over to death. This makes Jesus' kindness to Judas all the more extraordinary.

It's almost impossible to comprehend how hard it would have been for Jesus to be rejected by the world, and face death on a cross. But perhaps his betrayal by Judas gives us a way in to something of the emotion he would have felt. Being attacked by an enemy can hurt on the outside, but being betrayed by a loved one cuts us to the core of our being. Christ knows such experiences, and he feels their pain.

Today, as we look ahead to Easter and celebrating what Jesus achieved for us, spend a moment considering how costly this was. Ponder the 30 pieces of silver. Imagine the weight of them in your hand. Weigh them against Jesus' beautiful, righteous life. He was willing to be thought so little of. He became worthless in the world's eyes. And he did it because he loves us.

Prayer

O God, the Son of God –
  so loving, yet so hated
so forbearing, yet assaulted unto death
  who showed yourself so gentle and merciful to your persecutors;
grant that through the wounds of your passion
  our sins may be washed away,
and as in your humiliation you suffered death for us,
  so now, being glorified,
bestow on us everlasting brightness. Amen.
– Mozarabic liturgy (lightly modernised)

Song: *Oh the Deep, Deep Love of Jesus* **by Audrey Assad and Fernando Ortega**

38

DARK GETHSEMANE (MAUNDY THURSDAY)

When they hurled their insults at him, he did not retaliate; when he suffered, he made no threats. Instead, he entrusted himself to him who judges justly. 'He himself bore our sins' in his body on the cross, so that we might die to sins and live for righteousness; 'by his wounds you have been healed' (1 Peter 2:23–24).

Picture the scene in the Garden of Gethsemane on the Mount of Olives. Jesus has taken his disciples there after the Passover meal he has just shared with them. Jesus knows that he will be the Passover lamb, and his soul is crushed by the weight of this as he earnestly prays to the Father. Meanwhile, the disciples fall asleep, unable even to watch and pray with their master.

Then, torches appear on the hillside below. Soon, the clink of swords and spears can be heard as, out of the darkness, Judas appears, leading a group of soldiers. At this point the disciples are roused to action, with Peter even striking one of the servants with a sword. But Jesus faces the soldiers with calm and grace. The man of peace allows himself to be taken by men of war. The man who came to bring freedom allows himself to be put in chains. The light of the world allows himself to be swallowed up by darkness.

What would you have made of this scene if you had witnessed it, perhaps peering out from behind an olive tree? What would the look have been on Jesus' face?

Jesus made no threats. He did not retaliate. Despite being able to call down legions of angels, he made no attempt to defend himself. He entrusted himself to him who judges justly. This is what the anguished prayers and sweat like drops of blood had been about. Jesus' trust in his Father was hard won, and costly. There was nothing easy about Jesus going to the cross. *Nothing*. Perhaps we need to go to Gethsemane and spend some time there. Before we hear the triumphant cry from the cross: 'It is finished', we must first hear his cries of anguish. Before we see him in glory, we must first see him in the garden. This is our God. This is his love for you.

Prayer

> Lord Christ,
> A king, yet in chains
> A prophet, yet silent
> A priest, yet become the sacrifice
> Innocent, yet condemned
> Faithful friend, yet betrayed
> Creation's light, yet held in darkness
> True life, yet slain
> Lamb of God,
> We worship you.

Song: *Movement 3 (Isaiah 53:4–7)* **by The Corner Room**

39

IT IS FINISHED (GOOD FRIDAY)

He was pierced for our transgressions,
  he was crushed for our iniquities;
the punishment that brought us peace was on him,
  and by his wounds we are healed.
(**Isaiah 53:5**)

We've seen throughout these devotions the paradox of the Christian life that Jesus presents in the beatitudes. The way down is the way up. The way of giving is the way of receiving. Nowhere is this more exemplified than in the events of Jesus' execution. The way of death is the way of life.

Jesus, the righteous one, had never sinned, never hurt anyone, never spoke an unkind word, never had an impure thought. *This* Jesus was put to death as the worst of all criminals. He was persecuted, not just despite his righteousness, but *because* of it. 'This is the verdict: light has come into the world, but people loved darkness instead of light because their deeds were evil' (John 3:19).

If Lent is a season to take time to see ourselves rightly, then we must see ourselves in this damning verdict. We are not just the sheep who have gone astray, we are also the ones who sent Jesus the lamb to the slaughter. Easter gives us a sobering view of ourselves.

But we mustn't stop there. The purpose of seeing our sin is so that we may delight in our Saviour! Christ was pierced and crushed, so we might know healing and peace. Christ was forsaken by his Father, so that we might be embraced with open arms. Christ went out of the city and away from God, so that we might be welcomed in. Christ took upon himself our sin, so that we might put on his robes of righteousness. Christ died, that we might live.

Christ's words 'It is finished' tell us of the finality of what he achieved! There is now *no* condemnation for those who are in Christ Jesus. We can have complete confidence and a certain hope. Confession of sin is never the end of the story. It is not to lead us to despair, but to lead us to joy in the loving arms of our Saviour. Lent is not the end of the story. It is to prepare us for the joys of Easter!

Prayer

Jesus, light of the world
  You came to put an end to the darkness

  It is finished!

Jesus, the righteous one
  You came to bear all our sins and unrighteousness

  It is finished!

Jesus, beloved of the Father
  You were forsaken that we might be welcomed in

  It is finished!

Jesus, man of peace
  You died to put an end to all hostility

  It is finished!

Jesus, spotless lamb
  You were condemned, that we might face no condemnation

  It is finished!

Jesus, God of God
  You came to earth to open the gate of heaven

  It is finished!

Jesus, true Son of David
  You died as a criminal so you might reign in glory

  It is finished!

Jesus, source of all life
  You were laid in the tomb, so we might rise together with you.
  It is finished! Jesus, we worship you.

Song: *It Is Finished – Part II (Hark the voice of love and mercy)*
by Red Mountain Music

40

WAITING (HOLY SATURDAY)

Wait for the LORD;
   be strong and take heart
   and wait for the LORD.
(Psalm 27:14)

Picture the tomb on the that first Easter Saturday. Friday had been full of action and wonder. The trials, the crucifixion, Jesus' words 'It is finished!' and 'today you will be with me in paradise', the darkness of the sky, the temple curtain being torn, the dead saints rising from the graves.

But then the whole land falls silent. God falls silent. Jesus is in the grave. The Jewish people celebrate their day of rest, and perhaps God is resting too. And so we wait. All of creation waits. The sun rises and eventually sets, but it still feels like light has not dawned.

We are familiar with Good Friday and Easter Sunday: death and resurrection. But Easter Saturday also has much to teach us. It is a day of waiting. It pictures the whole of the Christian life. We live between Jesus' first coming (where he achieved salvation) and his second (where we fully experience all that he won for us). Of course, there are great joys in the Christian life now. We have eternal life now; we know the presence of God with us by his Spirit. But we are still 'those who wait'.

The whole of Lent is a picture of this waiting. Forty years in the wilderness before entering the promised land. Sowing in tears before reaping with joy. A seed being buried in the ground before bursting forth with much fruit. The 'downward way' that Jesus presents in the beatitudes as the way of flourishing. Waiting.

We know how the story continued for Jesus: the light of new creation that burst forth on resurrection Sunday. We know how the story will continue for us: we will share in that same future.

But for now, linger by the tomb on Easter Saturday. Feel the stillness. Feel the minutes and hours slowly pass. Wait, just as Jesus did.

Those who wait on the Lord will renew their strength. Those who join Jesus on the downward way, will rise with him in resurrection glory. Wait for the Lord. For in the morning, we rejoice.

Prayer

I cannot dance, Lord,
  unless you lead me.
If you want me to leap with abandon,
  You must intone the song.
Then I shall leap into love,
  From love into knowledge,
From knowledge into enjoyment,
  And from enjoyment beyond all human sensations.
There I want to remain,
  yet want also to circle
  higher still.
– Mechthild of Magdeburg

Song: *Those Who Wait* **by Matt Searles**

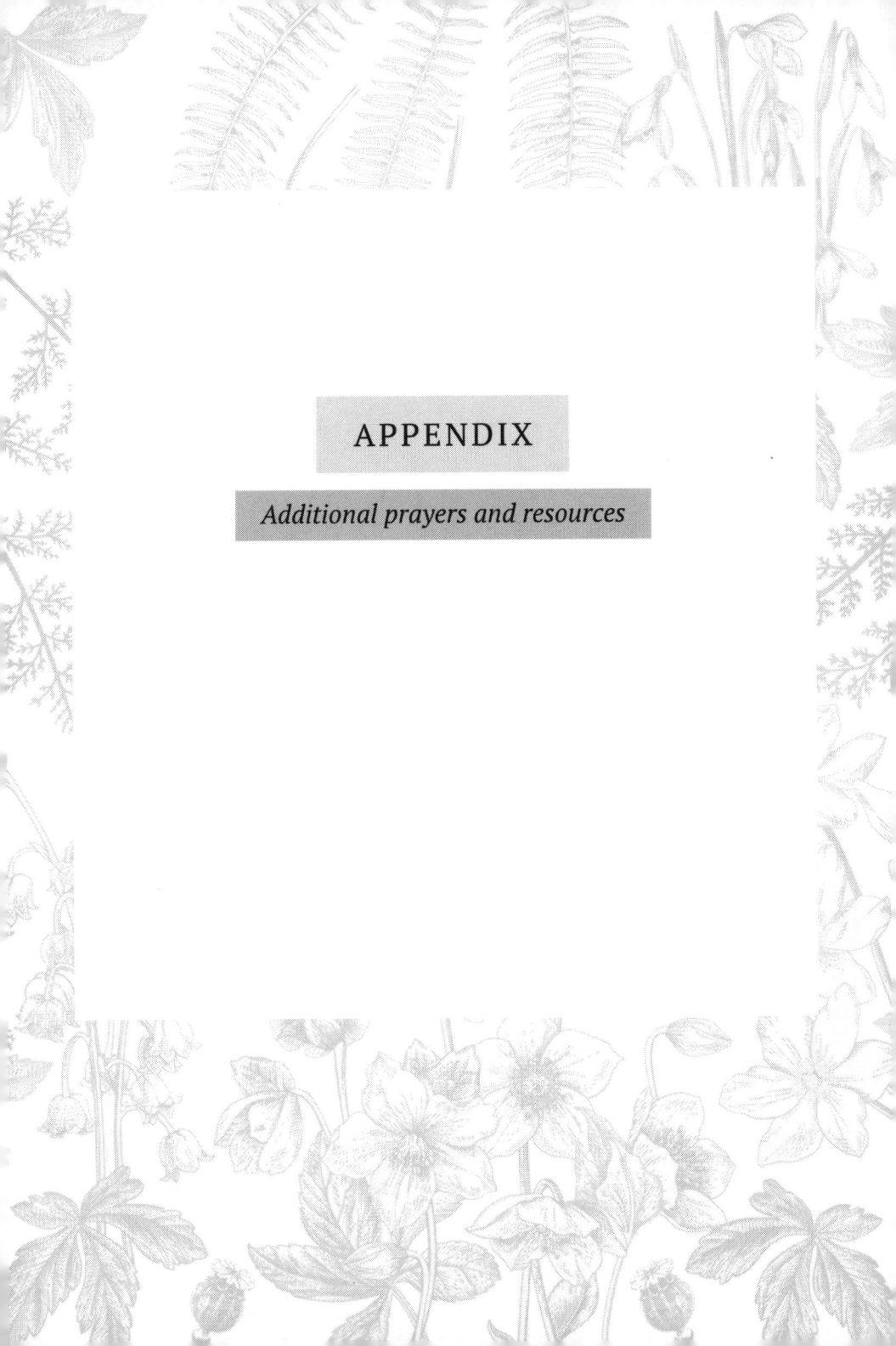

APPENDIX

Additional prayers and resources

BRIEF MORNING PRAYERS

You may wish to use one of the following prayers on busy mornings when time is too tight for a longer liturgy or devotional time.

Keep us safe, O God,
   as we take refuge in you.
Lead us in paths of righteousness
   for your name's sake.
(Adapted from Psalm 16:1 and Psalm 23:3)

May the grace of the Lord Jesus Christ,
and the love of God,
and the fellowship of the Holy Spirit
   be with us and all we love
   both today and for evermore.
(Adapted from 2 Corinthians 13:14)

Our Father in heaven,
hallowed be your name,
your kingdom come,
your will be done,
on earth as in heaven.
Give us today our daily bread.
Forgive us our sins
as we forgive those who sin against us.
Lead us not into temptation
but deliver us from evil.
For the kingdom, the power,
and the glory are yours
now and for ever.
Amen.
(The Lord's prayer – modern version)

We give you heartfelt thanks, O Lord,
  for the rest of the past night,
and the gift of a new day,
  with its many opportunities of pleasing you.
Grant that we may so pass its hours
  in the perfect freedom of your service,
that at eventide we may again give thanks to you;
  through Jesus Christ our Lord. Amen.
– From the daybreak service of the Eastern Church (third century)

Everlasting God, we give you thanks
  for the day and night just passed:
Gracious Father, for providing for us
  Blessed Son, for always being with us
  Holy Spirit, for directing and guiding us.
We lift to you the day ahead:
  with its joys and sorrows
  with our needs and plans.
May this be a day
  of listening to your voice
  of delighting in your Son
  and walking in the joy of the Holy Spirit.
Amen.

Bless all who worship you,
  from the rising of the sun
    to its setting.
Of your goodness, give us;
  with your love, inspire us;
by your spirit, guide us;
  by your power, protect us;
in your mercy, receive us
  now and always. Amen.
– An ancient collect (fifth century)

AN ALTERNATIVE DAILY PRAYER LITURGY

Y ou may choose to use this on any morning, or on the Sundays during Lent. However, as it is not Lent-specific, you may find this useful to use during the rest of the year.

Call to worship

It is good to praise the LORD
and make music to your name, O Most High,
proclaiming your love in the morning
and your faithfulness at night. (Psalm 92:1–2)

A moment's silence may be kept to prepare our hearts.

Opening prayer

Holy Spirit, giver of life,
be at work in us today:
Hold us fast to Christ,
direct our hearts to things above,
and lead us in paths of righteousness.
As you work in us for our infinite good,
may we rest in your comfort,
follow your promptings to obedience,
and delight in your assistance in prayer.
To the glory of God the Father
and Jesus Christ, in whose name we pray. Amen.

Bible reading

You may choose to read the psalm of the day (as set out in the table in the next chapter) or use a passage or devotional book of your choice.

Confession

If you, LORD, kept a record of sins,
LORD, who could stand?
But with you there is forgiveness,
so that we can, with reverence, serve you. (Psalm 130:3–4)

Silence may be kept for private confession of sin, or you may use one of the confession prayers from devotions 1, 3, 4, 8 or 29.

Words of assurance

> Who is a God like you,
> > who pardons sin and forgives transgression?
> You do not stay angry for ever
> > but delight to show mercy.
> You have compassion on us;
> You tread our sins underfoot
> > and hurl all our iniquities into the depths of the sea.
> For Christ suffered once for sins,
> > the righteous for the unrighteous, to bring us to God.
> **(Adapted from Micah 7:18–19 and 1 Peter 3:18)**

Prayer for the day ahead

> Father of all goodness,
> > who richly provides for all his children;
> we look to you for all we need today,
> > for apart from you we can do nothing.
> Grant us food in our stomachs
> > clothes on our backs
> breath in our lungs
> > and joy in our hearts.
> As the sun rises and gives light to all
> > so shine upon us the beams of your grace,
> that we may walk in the light of your presence
> > and be warmed at the fires of your love.

Blessing

> The LORD bless us
> > and keep us;
> the LORD make his face shine on us
> > and be gracious to us;
> the LORD turn his face towards us
> > and give us peace.
> **(Adapted from Numbers 6:24–26)**

PSALM OF THE DAY

The following table gives a psalm for each day of the month. There is great benefit in re-reading and getting to know certain parts of Scripture. Coming back to the same psalms each month might be a way of having some 'green pastures' in the Scriptures: passages that you know well, that become familiar friends.

During the Lent season, you might wish to use this plan on the Sundays, which are not technically part of the 40 days of Lent and so it is expected you'll pause the regular devotions. But you might wish to use this reading plan once Lent has finished, whether that is year-round, just for a season, or for any time you have that 'what should I read for my devotion today?' moment.

The psalms chosen below are not intended to be comprehensive, nor are they necessarily the 'most important' psalms. Rather, I have chosen psalms that I think lend themselves well to being read regularly in the context of daily prayer.

Day of month	Psalm	Day of month	Psalm
1	1	16	90
2	16	17	91
3	19	18	95
4	23	19	96
5	27	20	100
6	32	21	103
7	33	22	113
8	34	23	116
9	37	24	121
10	46	25	130
11	61	26	138
12	62	27	139
13	63	28	145
14	72	29	146
15	84	30	147
		31	119 (choose one or two sections)

A BEDTIME LITURGY

These prayers became favourite ones in our family, and we have used them with our daughter for years (with an optional high five and 'that's good news!' inserted after the assurance of forgiveness!). We found that, once we had used them for a few weeks, we had memorised them. We tend to say everything together, apart from the prayer of thanksgiving where we alternate the speaker line by line. When we say our own prayers of thanks, we do this out loud, but say the prayers of repentance silently. Please use them, though, in whatever way is most helpful to you.

Thanksgiving

>Give thanks to the LORD, for he is good.
>>His love endures for ever.
>Give thanks to the God of gods.
>>His love endures for ever.
>Give thanks to the Lord of lords:
>>His love endures for ever. **(Psalm 136:1–3)**

Time for personal prayers of thanks.

Confession

>Search me, God, and know my heart;
>>test me and know my anxious thoughts.
>See if there is any offensive way in me,
>>and lead me in the way everlasting. **(Psalm 139:23–24)**

Time for personal prayers of repentance.

Assurance of forgiveness

>[God] does not treat us as our sins deserve
>>or repay us according to our iniquities.
>For as high as the heavens are above the earth,
>>so great is his love for those who fear him;
>as far as the east is from the west,
>>so far has he removed our transgressions from us. **(Psalm 103:10–12)**

Conclusion

>In peace I will both lie down and sleep,
>>for you alone, O LORD, make me dwell in safety. **(Psalm 4:8 ESV)**

EXAMEN PRAYER

The Examen prayer dates back to St Ignatius of Loyola, and involves taking time at the end of the day to reflect on the day that has past, and in particular to do so thinking about how we have been walking (or not) in God's presence. This prayer tends to follow five steps as set out below.

1. Be aware of God's presence. As we review our day, we remember that we do so in God's presence, and his Fatherly embrace.

2. Give thanks. Are there particular things, whether big or small, that we can thank God for from today?

3. Review the day. For each part of the day, remember what you were doing, who you interacted with. Were you aware of God's presence with you at that time in the day? Were you walking closely with him? Were you turning away from him or ignoring him?

You may wish to review the day from morning to night, or to consider the day under these topical headings:

	or	
· Your waking		· What brought me joy
· Your morning		· What I found challenging
· Your lunchtime		· Times I stopped and paused
· Your afternoon		for reflection
· Your ending of work		· How I was aware of God's
· Your evening meal		presence in all this

4. Repentance and faith. Say sorry to God for times you have not walked with him, and delight afresh in his full forgiveness in Christ.

5. Look forward with hope. As we look to tomorrow, know that, whatever we face, God will be with us. Ask for his help to be aware of this glorious reality.

HEAVENLY MEDITATION

'Heavenly meditation' – meditating on the glories to come in the new creation – was a regular practice for Christian disciples a few centuries ago, but it may be unfamiliar to us. Running through the following acrostic could be useful in beginning our meditations on heaven, by giving us a structure. One minute spent meditating on each of these truths would lead to a meditation of nearly ten minutes.

J **Jesus will be there**
We will see him face to face.

E **End of sorrow and suffering**
Both in our lives, and in the lives of fellow Christians.

R **Renewed creation**
We will live in the new heavens and new earth, in all its splendour.

U **Undeserved**
We will know that we deserve condemnation, and we are only there by Christ's blood.

S **Sinless**
We will no longer sin, offending God and hurting others.

A **Adoring God perfectly**
We will finally love God as we should, and we will spend eternity praising him.

L **Loved**
We will finally understand and experience just how much he loves and has loved us.

E **Everlasting**
There will be no prospect of losing glory – we will be there in perfection forever.

M **Multitude**
There will be people from all nations, a new society, joyfully serving God together.

PRACTICE OF SILENCE ('MICRO-SABBATH')

Be still before the LORD (Psalm 37:7).

I have calmed and quieted myself,
    I am like a weaned child with its mother;
    like a weaned child I am content.
(Psalm 131:2)

Devotion to God will involve times of listening to him as we read Scripture, times of talking to him as we pray, but can also involve times of just being still in his presence, as the two psalms above encourage. This can feel very uncomfortable if we are used to being busy, with active minds the whole time. But moments of silence and stillness can be 'micro-sabbaths' as we stop and rest in God's presence. We can do so, knowing that he (not us) is in control, and is holding our salvation and our future. We can stop and be still, because God is always watching over us. Why not take a 'micro-sabbath' (maybe three minutes to begin with) when you just stop and rest in God's presence. The goal is not to meditate on God (good though that is) as this could be an excuse for our busy brain to get busy again. Nor is the goal to 'empty the mind'. Rather just stop and rest in God's presence, like the contented baby resting in her mother's arms.

- Sit in silence, aware of God's presence
- If thoughts come, choose to let them pass by without engaging with them
- Conclude by thanking God that we can stop and be still, because he is always watching over us

NOTES AND ACKNOWLEDGMENTS

I have quoted numerous prayers in this book from Christians throughout the centuries. Because of Lent's connection to the early church, I have sought in particular to draw prayers from the early church and the Middle Ages, which may be less well known than prayers from the modern period. Many of the prayers are drawn from two books that are freely available online:

- *Prayers of the Early Church*, edited by J. Manning Potts
- *Prayers of the Middle Ages*, edited by J. Manning Potts

Prayers by women were under-represented in these books, so I had to work harder to find these, mostly from online sources. For all the prayers, I have modernised the language and edited them for length. Any prayers with no author listed are my own.

For further reading on the beatitudes, the two best books I've used are:

- *The Message of the Sermon on the Mount* by John Stott (new edition: IVP, 2020; first published 1978)
- *The Beatitudes through the Ages* by Rebekah Eklund (William B. Eerdmans, 2021)

With thanks to Toni Searles, Heidi Johnston, Phil Sweeting, Andy Robinson and Dan Steel for their helpful comments on the manuscript as I was writing this book.

REFERENCES

1. Richard Baxter, *The Saints' Everlasting Rest* (Christian Heritage, 2001), p. 628.

2. John Stott, *The Message of the Sermon on the Mount (Matthew 5–7): Christian Counter-Culture*, The Bible Speaks Today (IVP, 1985), pp. 45–46.

3. The hymn 'The sands of time are sinking' by Samuel Rutherford and A.R. Cousin.

4. Andrew Bonar, *Memoir and Remains of the Rev. Robert Murray McCheyne* (1894), p. 293.

5. https://www.desiringgod.org/articles/celebrating-diversity-in-our-homes

6. Rebekah Eklund, *The Beatitudes through the Ages* (William B Eerdmans, 2021), pp. 253–4.

More books from 10Publishing

Resources that point to Jesus

10 Publishing
a division of **10** of those.com